High Protein Instant Pot Recipes With Original Photos for Every Dish!

⟷

72 Delicious Healthy Fit Lifestyle Meals Ideas

By Ava Mitchell

Copyright © 2023 by Ava Mitchell

Introduction

Are you on the hunt for high-protein meals that satisfy your taste buds and align with your health and fitness goals? Imagine having a collection of recipes right at your fingertips, specifically designed for the convenience of the Instant Pot, each accompanied by an inspiring, mouth-watering photo.

I bring you an extensive collection of 72 delectable dishes thoughtfully crafted for those who prioritize taste and health. I understand the challenge of balancing a busy life with the pursuit of a fit lifestyle. That's why each recipe is not just high in protein but also quick and easy to make, ensuring you never have to compromise on your diet or time.

Picture yourself whipping up meals like zesty lime chicken bowls, creamy lentil soups, or spicy beef stir-fry, all in record time. Imagine the aroma of freshly cooked meals filling your home after a long day, with the assurance that you're feeding your body with the high-protein nourishment it craves. With every page, you'll find original photos capturing the essence and allure of each dish. These images serve as a visual treat and a testament to what you can achieve in your kitchen.

Dive into this culinary journey with me and transform your Instant Pot cooking experience. Say goodbye to the monotony of repetitive meals and hello to a world where every dish explores taste and health. Whether you're a fitness enthusiast, a busy professional, or someone just starting on a healthy journey, this book is your ticket to mastering the art of high-protein cooking with the unmatched convenience of the Instant Pot. It's time to elevate your meals and nourish your body how it deserves!

Equip your kitchen with "High Protein Instant Pot Recipes With Original Photos for Every Dish!" and make every meal an unforgettable experience.

Table of Contents

High Protein Instant Pot Recipes offer a new and effective way to prepare delicious meals that support muscle growth, weight loss, and overall health. Let's delve into the world of these recipes, understanding their many advantages, the few downsides, and some added points to ponder.

Benefits of High Protein Instant Pot Recipes:

1. **Muscle Growth and Maintenance**: A high protein intake can aid muscle growth when combined with resistance training. It also helps prevent muscle loss, especially during weight loss or aging.
2. **Weight Loss and Satiety**: Protein-rich foods can make you feel fuller for longer. They can increase metabolism slightly and decrease overall calorie intake, aiding in weight loss.
3. **Quick Cooking Time**: The Instant Pot's pressure-cooking feature dramatically reduces cooking time. Especially beneficial for proteins that might take a long time to cook, like specific cuts of meat or beans.
4. **Preservation of Nutrients**: The Instant Pot requires less water than traditional cooking methods, meaning nutrients are leached out of the food during cogging.
5. **Pot Meals**: Most Instant Pot recipes are one-pot meals, meaning fewer dishes to wash and a more straightforward cooking process.
6. **Consistency**: The Instant Pot offers a controlled environment, which means your high-protein recipes will have consistent results every time.
7. **Versatility**: From beans and lentils to meats and poultry, you can prepare various protein sources using an Instant Pot.
8. **Safety Features**: Modern Instant Pots come with multiple safety features, reducing the risk of accidents during pressure cooking.
9. **Energy Efficient**: Using an Instant Pot can save energy compared to using an oven or a stovetop for extended periods.

Cons of High Protein Instant Pot Recipes:

1. **Learning Curve**: There might be a learning curve for those new to pressure cooking. It might take a few tries to get the timing and settings right.

2. **Initial Cost**: A good quality Instant Pot can be an investment upfront, though many argue it pays off in the long run due to its versatility.

3. **Size and Storage**: Storing the Instant Pot can be challenging for small kitchens due to its size.

4. **Not Always "Instant"**: While the Instant Pot cooks quickly, it takes time to come to and release pressure. This added time is sometimes not accounted for in recipes.

In conclusion, High Protein Instant Pot Recipes are an asset to anyone's culinary repertoire. Whether aiming for muscle growth, weight loss, or a delicious and nutritious meal, the Instant Pot can be your trusty ally.

Recipe 01: Quinoa Oat Granola Coconut Yogurt Bowl

SERVINGS: 4

PREPPING TIME: 15 MINUTES

COOK TIME: 20 MINUTES

DIFFICULTY: EASY

Energize your mornings with this delectable quinoa oat granola bowl! Paired with coconut yogurt, fresh fruit, seeds, and nuts high-protein breakfast is both nutritious and delightful, all made effortless with your Instant Pot.

Ingredients:

- ✓ 1 cup quinoa, rinsed and drained
- ✓ 1 cup rolled oats
- ✓ 2 cups coconut yogurt
- ✓ 1/2 cup mixed seeds (chia, flaxseed, pumpkin)
- ✓ 1/2 cup mixed nuts (almonds, walnuts, cashews)
- ✓ 1 cup fresh berries (blueberries, strawberries, raspberries)
- ✓ 2 ripe bananas, sliced
- ✓ 1/4 cup honey or to taste
- ✓ 1 cup freshly brewed coffee (optional)

Step-by-Step Preparation:

1. Combine quinoa, oats, and 2 cups of water in the Instant Pot. Cook on high pressure for 10 minutes, then quickly release.
2. Transfer the cooked quinoa-oat mixture to a bowl and allow to cool.
3. Take in serving bowls, layer quinoa-oat mixture, coconut yogurt, seeds, nuts, and fresh fruit.
4. Drizzle with honey to taste.
5. Serve immediately with a hot cup of coffee on the side, if desired.

Nutritional Facts: (Per serving)

- ❖ Calories: 400
- ❖ Protein: 15g
- ❖ Carbs: 55g
- ❖ Fats: 18g
- ❖ Fiber: 8g
- ❖ Sugars: 20g

Fuel your day with this nourishing breakfast bowl, packed with protein and natural sweetness. Whether preparing for a busy day ahead or enjoying a leisurely morning, this quinoa oat granola bowl promises a delightful and healthy start, all in the comfort of your kitchen.

Recipe 02: Mini Quiches With Spinach Quiche Florentine

SERVINGS: 6

PREPPING TIME: 15 MINUTES

COOK TIME: 12 MINUTES

DIFFICULTY: MEDIUM

These Mini Quiches with Spinach - Quiche Florentine - are a high-protein treat, perfect for a wholesome breakfast or a delightful brunch. Made effortlessly in the Instant Pot, their creamy texture complements the fresh burst of spinach and rich cheese. An excellent start to any day!

Ingredients:

- ✓ 1 cup fresh spinach, chopped
- ✓ 5 large eggs
- ✓ 1/4 cup heavy cream
- ✓ 1/2 cup grated cheddar cheese
- ✓ 1/4 cup feta cheese, crumbled
- ✓ 1/4 tsp salt
- ✓ 1/8 tsp black pepper
- ✓ 1/4 tsp nutmeg
- ✓ 2 tbsp olive oil
- ✓ 1 small onion, finely chopped

Step-by-Step Preparation:

1. Start the Instant Pot on sauté mode and add olive oil.
2. Add chopped onion and sauté until translucent.
3. Add chopped spinach and sauté just until wilted.
4. Whisk together eggs, heavy cream, salt, pepper, and nutmeg in a mixing bowl.
5. Stir in cheddar and feta cheese.
6. Pour the egg mixture over the sautéed spinach and onion in the Instant Pot.
7. Seal the lid and set it to manual pressure cook for 12 minutes.
8. Once done, allow for a natural release for 5 minutes, then a quick release.
9. Serve warm.

Nutritional Facts: (Per serving)

- ❖ Calories: 200
- ❖ Protein: 12g
- ❖ Fat: 15g
- ❖ Carbohydrates: 3g
- ❖ Fiber: 0.5g
- ❖ Sugar: 1g
- ❖ Sodium: 240mg

Elevate your breakfast game with these Mini Quiches infused with the wholesome goodness of Spinach Florentine. Packed with protein and cooked to perfection in an Instant Pot, these quiches are delicious and a nutrient powerhouse. Serve with a side salad or fresh fruit for a complete meal. Enjoy!

Recipe 03: Chicken Sausage and Hash Browns With Poached Egg

SERVINGS: 2

PREPPING TIME: 10 MINUTES

COOK TIME: 25 MINUTES

DIFFICULTY: EASY

Delight in the protein-packed goodness of "Chicken Sausage and Hash Browns with Poached Egg," a delicious Instant Pot breakfast. This recipe balances flavor and nutrition effortlessly.

Ingredients:

- ✓ 2 chicken sausage links
- ✓ 2 cups frozen hash browns
- ✓ 2 eggs
- ✓ 1 cup water
- ✓ Salt and pepper to taste
- ✓ Chopped parsley for garnish

Step-by-Step Preparation:

1. Set Instant Pot to sauté mode. Add chicken sausages and cook until browned. Remove and set aside.

2. Add hash browns to the pot, and saute until golden.

3. Return sausages to the pot, and add water, salt, and pepper.

4. Place a trivet over the mixture, and crack eggs onto it.

5. Seal Instant Pot and cook on high pressure for 3 minutes.

6. Perform a quick release, garnish with parsley.

Nutritional Facts: (Per serving)

- ❖ Calories: 320
- ❖ Protein: 23g
- ❖ Carbs: 18g
- ❖ Fat: 18g
- ❖ Fiber: 2g

Indulge in this nourishing breakfast that's effortlessly prepared using an Instant Pot. It's a savory delight to kickstart your day!

Recipe 04: Steel Cut Oats With Fresh Fruit and Honey

SERVINGS: 4

PREPPING TIME: 5 MINUTES

COOK TIME: 25 MINUTES

DIFFICULTY: EASY

Start your day with a nutritious boost! This steel-cut oats recipe, cooked perfectly in an Instant Pot, is paired with fresh fruits and a drizzle of honey. A high-protein breakfast that's delicious and time-efficient makes mornings more manageable and healthier.

Ingredients:

- ✓ 1 cup steel-cut oats
- ✓ 2.5 cups water
- ✓ Pinch of salt
- ✓ 1/2 cup mixed fresh fruits (berries, banana slices, etc.)
- ✓ 4 tablespoons honey
- ✓ Optional: 1/4 cup chopped nuts (like almonds or walnuts) for added protein

Step-by-Step Preparation:

1. Add steel-cut oats, water, and salt to the Instant Pot.
2. Close the lid and set the Instant Pot to 'Manual' or 'Pressure Cook' mode for 15 minutes.
3. Once done, allow the pressure to release naturally for 10 minutes, then perform a quick release.
4. Scoop out the cooked oats into bowls.
5. Top with fresh fruits, a drizzle of honey, and optional chopped nuts.
6. Stir gently, serve warm, and enjoy!

Nutritional Facts: (Per serving)

- ❖ Calories: 220 kcal
- ❖ Protein: 7g
- ❖ Carbohydrates: 39g
- ❖ Dietary Fiber: 5g
- ❖ Sugars: 12g (from fruits and honey)
- ❖ Fat: 3g (if adding nuts, adjust accordingly)

Elevate your breakfast game with this steel-cut oats recipe. The combination of hearty oats, fresh fruits, and the sweetness of honey is a delight. With the Instant Pot doing most of the work, you get a protein-packed breakfast that fuels your day without spending hours in the kitchen. Enjoy a wholesome start with minimal effort!

Recipe 05: Tofu Scramble With Greens Toast

SERVINGS: 4

PREPPING TIME: 10 MINUTES

COOK TIME: 15 MINUTES

DIFFICULTY: EASY

Jumpstart your day with this nutritious and delectable Tofu Scramble With Greens Toast. Made effortlessly in the Instant Pot, this protein-rich breakfast will energize you throughout the day.

Ingredients:

- ✓ 1 block (14 oz) of firm tofu, crumbled
- ✓ 2 tbsp olive oil
- ✓ 1 small onion, diced
- ✓ 1 bell pepper, chopped
- ✓ 2 cups mixed greens (spinach, kale, chard)
- ✓ 1 tsp turmeric (for color)
- ✓ Salt and pepper, to taste
- ✓ 4 slices of whole-grain toast
- ✓ 1/4 cup nutritional yeast (optional)

Step-by-Step Preparation:

1. Turn on the Instant Pot to the sauté setting and add olive oil.
2. Once hot, add onions and bell pepper, sautéing until softened.
3. Add the crumbled tofu, turmeric, salt, and pepper. Stir well.
4. Add mixed greens and sauté until wilted.
5. Sprinkle with nutritional yeast, if using, and give it a quick stir.
6. Toast your slices of bread.
7. Serve the tofu scramble atop the toasted slices.

Nutritional Facts: (Per serving)

- ❖ Calories: 280
- ❖ Protein: 18g
- ❖ Carbs: 25g
- ❖ Fat: 12g
- ❖ Fiber: 5g
- ❖ Sugar: 3g
- ❖ Sodium: 320mg

Elevate your morning routine with this sumptuous Tofu Scramble With Greens Toast. Whether hitting the gym or heading to work, this high-protein breakfast ensures you start your day on the right foot. Enjoy the burst of flavors and nutrients!

Recipe 06: Lentil Porridge With a Sprig of Basil

SERVINGS: 4

PREPPING TIME: 10 MINUTES

COOK TIME: 25 MINUTES

DIFFICULTY: EASY

Dive into a hearty and nutritious breakfast that combines the rich protein of lentils with the fresh touch of basil. This Instant Pot dish is perfect for busy mornings, ensuring you energize your day.

Ingredients:

- ✓ 1 cup dried lentils, rinsed and drained
- ✓ 4 cups water
- ✓ 1/2 teaspoon salt
- ✓ 1 tablespoon olive oil
- ✓ 1/4 cup chopped onions
- ✓ 2 garlic cloves, minced
- ✓ A handful of fresh basil leaves
- ✓ 1/4 teaspoon black pepper
- ✓ Optional toppings: sliced almonds, honey, or a dollop of yogurt

Step-by-Step Preparation:

1. Set the Instant Pot to Saute mode. Add olive oil, onions, and garlic. Cook until onions are translucent.
2. Add lentils, water, and salt. Stir well.
3. Close the lid and set the Instant Pot to 'Manual' or 'Pressure Cook' for 20 minutes.
4. Allow the pressure to release naturally.
5. Open the lid, stir in the fresh basil and black pepper.
6. Serve hot, garnished with your choice of toppings.

Nutritional Facts: (Per serving)

- ❖ Calories: 210
- ❖ Protein: 13g
- ❖ Carbohydrates: 35g
- ❖ Dietary Fiber: 15g
- ❖ Sugars: 2g
- ❖ Fat: 3.5g
- ❖ Sodium: 310mg

Indulge in the wholesome goodness of lentils, elevated by the aromatic touch of basil. Whether to fuel your morning workout or crave a satisfying start, this lentil porridge is a delectable choice. Healthy eating has never been this delightful!

Recipe 07: Burrito Flour Tortilla With Chili Con Carne Filling

SERVINGS: 4

PREPPING TIME: 20 MINUTES

COOK TIME: 25 MINUTES

DIFFICULTY: INTERMEDIATE

Wake up to a vibrant fusion of flavors with this high-protein Instant Pot breakfast burrito. Combining the rich essence of Mexican and Tex-Mex cuisines, this dish wraps chili con carne in a soft flour tortilla, offering a hearty start to your day.

Ingredients:

- 4 large flour tortillas
- 1 lb lean ground beef
- 1 can (15 oz) black beans, drained and rinsed
- 1 cup cheddar cheese, shredded
- 1 onion, finely chopped
- 2 garlic cloves, minced
- 1 can (10 oz) diced tomatoes with green chilies
- 1 tsp ground cumin
- 1 tsp chili powder
- Salt and pepper to taste
- Fresh cilantro for garnish
- Sour cream for serving (optional)

Step-by-Step Preparation:

1. Turn on the Instant Pot and set it to "Sauté" mode. Add the ground beef, breaking it apart as it cooks.

2. Once the beef is browned, add onions and garlic. Cook until translucent.

3. Add beans, diced tomatoes with chilies, cumin, chili powder, salt, and pepper. Stir to combine.

4. Close the lid, set to "Manual" mode, and cook for 10 minutes on high pressure.

5. Once done, perform a quick release and stir the chili con carne mixture.

6. Warm the tortillas and place a generous amount of the filling in each, topping with cheese.

7. Roll the tortillas to form burritos. If desired, serve with a sprinkle of cilantro and a dollop of sour cream.

Nutritional Facts: (Per serving)

- Calories: 550
- Protein: 35g
- Carbohydrates: 45g
- Dietary Fiber: 7g
- Total Fat: 25g
- Saturated Fat: 10g
- Cholesterol: 90mg
- Sodium: 750mg

Indulge in this sumptuous Instant Pot breakfast burrito, uniting the robust flavors of Mexico and Tex-Mex in every bite. It's not just a meal; it's a delightful culinary journey that sets the right tone for the rest of your day. Enjoy every protein-packed bite!

Recipe 08: Chocolate Chia Overnight Oats

SERVINGS: 4

PREPPING TIME: 10 MINUTES

COOK TIME: 4 HOURS (OVERNIGHT)

DIFFICULTY: EASY

Kickstart your day with a delicious and nutritious bowl of Chocolate Chia Overnight Oats. This high-protein Instant Pot breakfast dish perfectly blends creamy oats, chia seeds, and rich chocolate.

Ingredients:

- ✓ 2 cups rolled oats
- ✓ 3 cups almond milk
- ✓ 1/4 cup chia seeds
- ✓ 1/4 cup unsweetened cocoa powder
- ✓ 2 tablespoons honey or maple syrup
- ✓ 1 teaspoon vanilla extract
- ✓ Pinch of salt
- ✓ Toppings of choice (berries, nuts, etc.)

Step-by-Step Preparation:

1. Combine the oats, chia seeds, cocoa powder, honey, vanilla extract, and salt in a bowl.
2. Pour the mixture into the Instant Pot.
3. Add almond milk and stir to combine.
4. Cover and set the Instant Pot to the "Yogurt" setting. Let it sit overnight or for at least 4 hours.
5. In the morning, give the mixture a good stir. Adjust sweetness if needed.
6. Serve in bowls and top with your favorite toppings.

Nutritional Facts: (Per serving)

- ❖ Calories: 220
- ❖ Protein: 7g
- ❖ Carbohydrates: 34g
- ❖ Dietary Fiber: 8g
- ❖ Sugars: 8g
- ❖ Fat: 7g
- ❖ Sodium: 80mg

Indulge in a breakfast that's not only delectable but also packed with energy-boosting nutrients. With the convenience of the Instant Pot, this Chocolate Chia Overnight Oats recipe promises a healthy and delightful start to your mornings. Enjoy and energize!

Recipe 09: Pumpkin Chia Seed Pudding

SERVINGS: 4

PREPPING TIME: 10 MINUTES

COOK TIME: 20 MINUTES

DIFFICULTY: EASY

Start your day with a nutritious and protein-packed breakfast! This Pumpkin Chia Seed Pudding made in an Instant Pot is delicious and loaded with essential nutrients to fuel your morning.

Ingredients:

- ✓ 1 cup pumpkin puree
- ✓ 2 cups almond milk (or any milk of your choice)
- ✓ 1/2 cup chia seeds
- ✓ 3 tablespoons maple syrup or honey
- ✓ 1 teaspoon vanilla extract
- ✓ 1/2 teaspoon cinnamon
- ✓ 1/4 teaspoon nutmeg
- ✓ A pinch of salt
- ✓ 4 tablespoons protein powder (optional)

Step-by-Step Preparation:

1. Combine pumpkin puree, almond milk, maple syrup, vanilla extract, cinnamon, nutmeg, and salt in the Instant Pot. Mix well.
2. Stir in the chia seeds and protein powder (if using) until well combined.
3. Secure the Instant Pot lid and set the pressure to 'Low' for 20 minutes.
4. Once cooked, release the pressure naturally and then carefully open the lid.
5. Stir the pudding, ensuring a smooth consistency.
6. Transfer the pudding into bowls and refrigerate for 2 hours or until set.
7. Serve chilled with your favorite toppings!

Nutritional Facts: (Per serving)

- ❖ Calories: 210 kcal
- ❖ Protein: 12g
- ❖ Carbs: 25g
- ❖ Dietary Fiber: 8g
- ❖ Sugars: 10g
- ❖ Fat: 8g
- ❖ Saturated Fat: 1g
- ❖ Sodium: 90mg

Reinvent your breakfast routine with this Pumpkin Chia Seed Pudding! It promises to be a hit with both adults and kids, a delightful blend of flavors with the added goodness of chia and pumpkin. Easy to make and perfect for busy mornings, it's the ideal breakfast to kickstart your day.

Recipe 10: Ham and Egg Omelette

SERVINGS: 2

PREPPING TIME: 10 MINUTES

COOK TIME: 5 MINUTES

DIFFICULTY: EASY

Kickstart your day with a nourishing ham and egg omelet made with bio eggs, garnished with fresh herbs, and accompanied by a crisp salad. This recipe is prepared in an Instant Pot and promises a high-protein breakfast that'll keep you energized all morning.

Ingredients:

- ✓ 4 bio eggs
- ✓ 100g diced ham
- ✓ 1/4 cup chopped fresh herbs (parsley, chives, and basil)
- ✓ 1/2 cup mixed salad greens (lettuce, spinach, arugula)
- ✓ 1 tbsp olive oil
- ✓ Salt and pepper to taste
- ✓ 1/4 cup grated cheese (optional)
- ✓ 2 tbsp water

Step-by-Step Preparation:

1. Whisk together the bio eggs, water, salt, and pepper in a bowl until well combined.
2. Stir in the diced ham and half of the fresh herbs.
3. Pour the mixture into a greased Instant Pot-safe dish.
4. Close the Instant Pot lid, set it to "Steam" mode, and cook for 5 minutes.
5. Once done, carefully release the pressure and open the lid.
6. Slide the omelet onto a plate, sprinkle the remaining fresh herbs, and serve with the mixed salad drizzled with olive oil.

Nutritional Facts: (Per serving)

- ❖ Calories: 280 kcal
- ❖ Protein: 22g
- ❖ Fat: 19g
- ❖ Carbohydrates: 3g
- ❖ Fiber: 1g
- ❖ Sugars: 1g

There's no better way to greet the morning than with a protein-packed, flavorful omelet made with bio eggs. This ham and egg omelet, garnished with vibrant herbs and paired with a fresh salad, is a delightful fusion of taste and health, ensuring a refreshing start to your day.

Recipe 11: Quiche With Chicken, Cherry Tomatoes and Cheese

SERVINGS: 4

PREPPING TIME: 15 MINUTES

COOK TIME: 25 MINUTES

DIFFICULTY: INTERMEDIATE

This savory Quiche with Chicken, Cherry Tomatoes, and Cheese, cooked to perfection in an Instant Pot, will elevate your brunch game. High in protein and bursting with flavor, it's an all-in-one meal that pairs well with fresh salads or toast.

Ingredients:

- ✓ 1 pre-made pie crust
- ✓ 1 cup cooked chicken, diced
- ✓ 1/2 cup cherry tomatoes, halved
- ✓ 1 cup cheddar cheese, grated
- ✓ 4 large eggs
- ✓ 1 cup milk or cream
- ✓ 1/4 tsp salt
- ✓ 1/4 tsp black pepper
- ✓ 2 tbsp fresh basil, chopped

Step-by-Step Preparation:

1. Place the pie crust into a suitable Instant Pot-friendly dish.
2. Scatter the diced chicken, cherry tomatoes, and half of the cheese onto the crust.
3. Whisk together the eggs, milk, salt, pepper, and basil in a bowl.
4. Pour the egg mixture over the chicken and tomatoes.
5. Sprinkle the remaining cheese on top.
6. Cover with aluminum foil.
7. Pour 1 cup of water into the Instant Pot. Place the dish on the trivet and lower it into the pot.
8. Seal the Instant Pot lid, set it to 'Manual' or 'Pressure Cook,' and cook for 25 minutes.
9. Once cooked, release the pressure naturally for 10 minutes, then vent to release any remaining pressure.
10. Remove the quiche and let it cool for a few minutes before serving.

Nutritional Facts: (Per serving)

- ❖ Calories: 410 kcal
- ❖ Protein: 26g
- ❖ Carbohydrates: 25g
- ❖ Dietary Fiber: 1g
- ❖ Sugars: 4g
- ❖ Fat: 24g
- ❖ Saturated Fat: 10g
- ❖ Sodium: 420mg

This Instant Pot Quiche offers a harmonious blend of chicken, tomatoes, and cheese, making brunches delightful and fulfilling. Whether entertaining guests or craving a hearty meal, this high-protein dish will be a surefire hit. Serve with your favorite sides and enjoy a gourmet experience from the comfort of your home.

Recipe 12: Shakshuka With Chickpeas

SERVINGS: 4

PREPPING TIME: 15 MINUTES

COOK TIME: 10 MINUTES

DIFFICULTY: INTERMEDIATE

Delight your taste buds with a high-protein brunch dish that effortlessly fuses robust flavors with nutritious elements. Shakshuka with Chickpeas, traditionally a North African dish, gets an instant pot twist, making it the perfect weekend brunch sensation.

Ingredients:

- ✓ 2 tablespoons olive oil
- ✓ 1 large onion, chopped
- ✓ 3 garlic cloves, minced
- ✓ 1 red bell pepper, chopped
- ✓ 1 can (14 oz) diced tomatoes
- ✓ 1 can (14 oz) chickpeas, drained and rinsed

- ✓ 2 teaspoons paprika
- ✓ 1 teaspoon cumin
- ✓ 1/4 teaspoon cayenne pepper
- ✓ Salt and pepper to taste
- ✓ 4 large eggs
- ✓ Fresh cilantro for garnish

Step-by-Step Preparation:

1. Turn on the instant pot's sauté mode and add olive oil. Once hot, add onion, garlic, and bell pepper, sautéing until softened.

2. Stir in the tomatoes, chickpeas, paprika, cumin, cayenne, salt, and pepper. Mix well.

3. Create four small wells in the mixture and gently crack an egg into each well.

4. Close the lid, set the pot to 'Manual' mode, and cook on high pressure for 5 minutes.

5. Quickly release the pressure, sprinkle with cilantro, and serve warm.

Nutritional Facts: (Per serving)

- ❖ Calories: 280 kcal
- ❖ Protein: 14g
- ❖ Carbohydrates: 30g
- ❖ Dietary Fiber: 8g
- ❖ Fats: 12g
- ❖ Sugars: 6g
- ❖ Sodium: 420mg

Shakshuka with Chickpeas isn't just a brunch staple; it's an experience. Warm, comforting, and teeming with protein, this dish is the ideal convergence of tradition and modernity. Next weekend, turn your brunch into an unforgettable culinary journey with this instant pot marvel.

Recipe 13: Lentil Spinach Soup

SERVINGS: 4

PREPPING TIME: 10 MINUTES

COOK TIME: 20 MINUTES

DIFFICULTY: EASY

Indulge in a nourishing bowl of Lentil Spinach Soup, a perfect harmony of protein and greens. This Instant Pot recipe ensures a quick yet delectable brunch option that will leave you satiated and energized.

Ingredients:

- ✓ 1 cup dried lentils, rinsed and drained
- ✓ 4 cups fresh spinach, chopped
- ✓ 1 medium onion, diced
- ✓ 2 garlic cloves, minced
- ✓ 1 medium carrot, chopped
- ✓ 1 tsp olive oil
- ✓ 1 tsp cumin powder
- ✓ 1/2 tsp turmeric powder
- ✓ 4 cups vegetable broth
- ✓ Salt and pepper to taste

Step-by-Step Preparation:

1. Set the Instant Pot to 'Sauté' mode and add olive oil.
2. Once hot, add the onions and garlic, sautéing until translucent.
3. Add carrots, cumin, and turmeric, and saute for 2 more minutes.
4. Stir in the lentils, spinach, and vegetable broth.
5. Close the lid, set the Instant Pot to 'Manual' mode, and cook for 15 minutes.
6. Allow natural pressure release.
7. Season with salt and pepper, stir well and serve hot.

Nutritional Facts: (Per serving)

- ❖ Calories: 220
- ❖ Protein: 15g
- ❖ Carbohydrates: 35g
- ❖ Dietary Fiber: 15g
- ❖ Sugars: 3g
- ❖ Fat: 2g
- ❖ Sodium: 150mg

Packed with the goodness of lentils and fresh spinach, this soup promises a healthy start to your day. It's not just a meal but a delightful experience celebrating nature's best offerings. Elevate your brunch moments with this heartwarming delicacy.

Recipe 14: Spaghetti With Meatballs

SERVINGS: 4

PREPPING TIME: 20 MINUTES

COOK TIME: 25 MINUTES

DIFFICULTY: MODERATE

Delight in a classic favorite reimagined for a high-protein brunch. This Instant Pot version of spaghetti with meatballs in a zesty tomato sauce promises to impress guests with flavor and nutrition in each bite, making brunch genuinely unforgettable.

Ingredients:

- ✓ 400 grams of spaghetti
- ✓ 500 grams of lean ground beef or turkey
- ✓ 1 cup of breadcrumbs
- ✓ 2 large eggs
- ✓ 1/4 cup grated Parmesan
- ✓ 2 cups of canned crushed tomatoes
- ✓ 3 cloves of garlic, minced
- ✓ 1/2 cup diced onions
- ✓ 1 tablespoon of olive oil
- ✓ 1 teaspoon dried oregano
- ✓ Salt and pepper, to taste
- ✓ Fresh basil for garnish

Step-by-Step Preparation:

1. Combine ground meat, breadcrumbs, eggs, Parmesan, salt, and pepper. Mix well and form into medium-sized meatballs.

2. Set the Instant Pot to "Saute" mode. Add olive oil, garlic, and onions, cooking until translucent.

3. Add the crushed tomatoes and oregano. Gently place meatballs in the sauce.

4. Close the Instant Pot lid and set to "Pressure Cook" on high for 15 minutes.

5. Quickly release the pressure. Stir in the spaghetti, ensuring it's submerged in the sauce.

6. Seal the Instant Pot lid and pressure cook for 8 minutes.

7. Quick release, garnish with fresh basil and serve hot.

Nutritional Facts: (Per serving)

- ❖ Calories: 580
- ❖ Protein: 35g
- ❖ Carbohydrates: 68g
- ❖ Fats: 18g
- ❖ Sodium: 450mg
- ❖ Dietary Fiber: 5g

Revel in the union of robust flavors and nourishing protein with this Instant Pot spaghetti and meatballs recipe. A twist on the traditional, it's a guaranteed crowd-pleaser and a seamless blend of convenience and health for the ultimate brunch dish.

Recipe 15: Bell Pepper Stuffed With a Turkey, Rice, Quinoa Mixture

SERVINGS: 4

PREPPING TIME: 20 MINUTES

COOK TIME: 15 MINUTES

DIFFICULTY: MEDIUM

Delight your taste buds with a high-protein, nutritious brunch: yellow bell peppers stuffed with a turkey, rice, and quinoa mixture. This delectable dish cooked in an Instant Pot ensures flavor and health, making your brunch special.

Ingredients:

- ✓ 4 yellow bell peppers, tops removed and hollowed out
- ✓ 1/2 lb ground turkey
- ✓ 1/2 cup cooked rice
- ✓ 1/2 cup cooked quinoa
- ✓ 1/4 cup diced onions
- ✓ 2 cloves garlic, minced
- ✓ 1 tbsp olive oil
- ✓ 1 tsp ground cumin
- ✓ Salt and pepper, to taste
- ✓ 1 cup tomato sauce (optional for added moisture)

Step-by-Step Preparation:

1. Set the Instant Pot to 'Sauté' mode and add olive oil.
2. Add onions and garlic, and saute until translucent.
3. Add ground turkey, cooking until browned.
4. Stir in rice, quinoa, cumin, salt, and pepper.
5. Stuff each bell pepper with the turkey mixture.
6. If using tomato sauce, pour it over the stuffed peppers.
7. Place the peppers in the Instant Pot, and secure the lid.
8. Set to 'Manual' mode and cook for 15 minutes.
9. Release pressure, open the lid, and serve hot.

Nutritional Facts: (Per serving)

- ❖ Calories: 280
- ❖ Protein: 20g
- ❖ Carbohydrates: 30g
- ❖ Fat: 8g
- ❖ Fiber: 5g
- ❖ Sugars: 6g
- ❖ Sodium: 220mg

Elevate your brunch game with these savory stuffed bell peppers. Packed with the goodness of turkey, rice, and quinoa is filling and flavorful. Whether you're serving it to family or guests, this dish will impress and leave everyone craving more.

Recipe 16: Mini Quiche Pie With Feta, Spinach and Pine Nuts

SERVINGS: 4

PREPPING TIME: 15 MINUTES

COOK TIME: 25 MINUTES

DIFFICULTY: MEDIUM

Experience the harmonious blend of feta, spinach, and pine nuts encased in a golden crust. This traditional mini quiche pie offers a high-protein punch perfect for your next brunch. Using an Instant Pot ensures a perfectly set filling every time.

Ingredients:

- ✓ 1 ready-made pie crust
- ✓ 3 large eggs
- ✓ 1 cup of feta cheese, crumbled
- ✓ 1 cup of fresh spinach, chopped
- ✓ 1/4 cup of pine nuts
- ✓ 1/4 cup of heavy cream
- ✓ Salt and pepper to taste
- ✓ 1 tbsp of olive oil

Step-by-Step Preparation:

1. Grease the Instant Pot's steaming dish with olive oil.
2. Roll out the pie crust and cut it into mini circles to fit the dish.
3. Whisk together eggs, heavy cream, salt, and pepper in a bowl.
4. Stir in the feta, spinach, and pine nuts.
5. Pour the mixture into the crusts, making sure not to overfill.
6. Set the Instant Pot to "Steam" mode and cook for 25 minutes.
7. Allow the quiche to cool slightly before serving.

Nutritional Facts: (Per serving)

- ❖ Calories: 320
- ❖ Protein: 12g
- ❖ Carbohydrates: 20g
- ❖ Fat: 22g
- ❖ Fiber: 1.5g
- ❖ Sugars: 2g
- ❖ Sodium: 300mg

Bite into the feta's creaminess, the egg's richness, and the crunchy touch of pine nuts with this delectable mini quiche. It's a delightful treat to elevate your brunch experience, ensuring each bite is a perfect symphony of flavors. Enjoy your high-protein dish in style!

Recipe 17: Chorizo Potato Hash With Eggs and Feta Cheese

SERVINGS: 4

PREPPING TIME: 15 MINUTES

COOK TIME: 20 MINUTES

DIFFICULTY: EASY

This hearty Chorizo Potato Hash with Eggs and Feta Cheese is the ultimate protein-packed brunch dish. Using the Instant Pot makes this meal quick, flavorful, and fuss-free, bringing the rich flavors of chorizo and the creaminess of feta together in one comforting dish.

Ingredients:

- ✓ 1 lb chorizo sausage, crumbled
- ✓ 3 medium-sized potatoes, diced
- ✓ 4 large eggs
- ✓ 1/2 cup feta cheese, crumbled
- ✓ 1/4 cup red bell pepper, diced
- ✓ 1 small onion, diced
- ✓ 2 cloves garlic, minced
- ✓ 2 tablespoons olive oil
- ✓ Salt and pepper, to taste
- ✓ Fresh parsley for garnish

Step-by-Step Preparation:

1. Turn the Instant Pot to sauté mode and heat olive oil. Add chorizo, cooking until browned.
2. Add onion, garlic, and bell pepper, sautéing until soft.
3. Stir in diced potatoes, seasoning with salt and pepper.
4. Close the Instant Pot lid and set it to manual pressure for 8 minutes.
5. Quick-release pressure and make four wells in the hash.
6. Crack an egg into each well.
7. Set the Instant Pot to sauté mode and cook until the eggs are set.
8. Sprinkle with feta cheese and garnish with fresh parsley.

Nutritional Facts: (Per serving)

- ❖ Calories: 520
- ❖ Protein: 28g
- ❖ Carbohydrates: 40g
- ❖ Fat: 28g
- ❖ Fiber: 5g
- ❖ Sodium: 790mg

This hash's delightful combination of spicy chorizo, tender potatoes, creamy eggs, and tangy feta makes it a brunch favorite. Prepared effortlessly in the Instant Pot, this dish promises nutrition and indulgence, ensuring your morning starts on a delicious and energetic note. Perfect for family gatherings or a relaxed weekend treat!

Recipe 18: Quesadilla With Vegetables and Cheese

SERVINGS: 4

PREPPING TIME: 10 MINUTES

COOK TIME: 15 MINUTES

DIFFICULTY: EASY

Indulge in a nutritious brunch with this high-protein Quesadilla packed with fresh vegetables and cheese. Cooked effortlessly in an Instant Pot, this dish promises taste and health in one bite.

Ingredients:

- ✓ 8 medium-sized tortillas
- ✓ 1 cup mixed bell peppers, finely chopped
- ✓ 1 cup zucchini, diced
- ✓ 1 cup corn kernels
- ✓ 1.5 cups shredded cheddar or Mexican blend cheese
- ✓ 1 teaspoon olive oil
- ✓ Salt and pepper, to taste
- ✓ 1 teaspoon chili powder (optional)
- ✓ ½ cup black beans drained and rinsed

Step-by-Step Preparation:

1. Turn the Instant Pot on Sauté mode and add olive oil.

2. Once hot, add the bell peppers, zucchini, and corn. Sauté for 3-4 minutes or until slightly tender.

3. Add salt, pepper, and chili powder. Stir well.

4. Lay out a tortilla, sprinkle with cheese, sauteed vegetables, black beans, and another layer of cheese. Top with a second tortilla.

5. Place the Quesadilla in the Instant Pot and close the lid. Set to Manual for 3 minutes.

6. Release pressure and carefully remove the Quesadilla.

7. Repeat with the remaining tortillas and fillings.

8. Serve hot with salsa or sour cream.

Nutritional Facts: (Per serving)

- ❖ Calories: 320
- ❖ Protein: 18g
- ❖ Carbohydrates: 35g
- ❖ Dietary Fiber: 6g
- ❖ Sugars: 4g
- ❖ Fat: 12g
- ❖ Sodium: 420mg

As you savor each bite of this scrumptious Quesadilla, let fresh veggies and melty cheese flavors dance on your palate. It is perfect for brunch or a quick snack and offers a delightful blend of taste, nutrition, and convenience. Reimagine brunch with this Instant Pot delicacy!

Recipe 19: Risotto With Cep Mushroom and Broccoli

SERVINGS: 4

PREPPING TIME: 15 MINUTES

COOK TIME: 20 MINUTES

DIFFICULTY: INTERMEDIATE

Delight your taste buds with this high-protein Risotto with Cep Mushroom and Broccoli. Perfectly creamy and nutritious, this Instant Pot brunch recipe is delicious, quick, and easy to whip up, making your mornings effortlessly gourmet.

Ingredients:

- ✓ 1 cup Arborio rice
- ✓ 2 cups fresh Cep mushrooms, sliced
- ✓ 1 cup broccoli florets
- ✓ 1 onion, finely chopped
- ✓ 2 cloves garlic, minced
- ✓ 4 cups vegetable broth
- ✓ ½ cup Parmesan cheese, grated
- ✓ 2 tbsp olive oil
- ✓ Salt and pepper, to taste
- ✓ 1 tsp fresh thyme

Step-by-Step Preparation:

1. Set the Instant Pot to 'Saute' and heat olive oil. Add onions and garlic, cooking until translucent.

2. Stir in Cep mushrooms and cook for 3-4 minutes.

3. Add Arborio rice, stirring constantly for 2 minutes.

4. Pour in vegetable broth, broccoli, thyme, salt, and pepper. Mix well.

5. Close the Instant Pot lid and set it to 'Pressure Cook' for 15 minutes.

6. Once done, release the pressure and open the lid.

7. Stir in Parmesan cheese until creamy, and serve.

Nutritional Facts: (Per serving)

- ❖ Calories: 300
- ❖ Protein: 12g
- ❖ Carbs: 45g
- ❖ Fat: 8g
- ❖ Fiber: 3g
- ❖ Sugars: 2g
- ❖ Sodium: 580mg

Elevate your brunch game with this Risotto with Cep Mushroom and Broccoli. High in protein and flavors, it's an impeccable blend of creamy rice, earthy mushrooms, and crunchy broccoli. Whether hosting a brunch or simply indulging on a lazy Sunday, this Instant Pot dish promises to impress every time.

Recipe 20: Beef Stew With Vegetables

SERVINGS: 4

PREPPING TIME: 20 MINUTES

COOK TIME: 45 MINUTES

DIFFICULTY: MEDIUM

An ideal brunch dish that blends the richness of beef with the wholesomeness of fresh vegetables. Cooked conveniently in an Instant Pot, this high-protein stew is a delicious fusion of flavors, making it both nutritious and comforting.

Ingredients:

- ✓ 500g beef chunks, cubed
- ✓ 2 cups beef broth
- ✓ 3 large carrots, sliced
- ✓ 2 potatoes, diced
- ✓ 1 onion, chopped
- ✓ 2 cloves garlic, minced
- ✓ 1 cup green peas
- ✓ 1 teaspoon salt
- ✓ 1/2 teaspoon pepper
- ✓ 2 tablespoons olive oil
- ✓ 1 teaspoon dried thyme
- ✓ 2 bay leaves

Step-by-Step Preparation:

1. Set the Instant Pot to 'Saute' mode and heat olive oil.
2. Add beef chunks and brown for about 5 minutes.
3. Add onions and garlic, and sauté until translucent.
4. Pour in beef broth and ensure the beef is submerged.
5. Add carrots, potatoes, peas, salt, pepper, thyme, and bay leaves.
6. Close the lid and set it to 'Manual' or 'Pressure Cook' on high for 35 minutes.
7. Once done, release pressure naturally for 10 minutes.
8. Adjust seasoning if needed and serve hot.

Nutritional Facts: (Per serving)

- ❖ Calories: 350
- ❖ Protein: 28g
- ❖ Carbohydrates: 26g
- ❖ Dietary Fiber: 5g
- ❖ Fats: 12g
- ❖ Sodium: 800mg

This Beef Stew with Vegetables is an exquisite brunch dish that promises a burst of flavor in every bite. Not only does it satisfy your taste buds, but it also fuels your body with essential nutrients. Savor it with some crusty bread on a lazy weekend morning, or enjoy it as a hearty weekday meal. Whatever the occasion, this dish is sure to impress!

←——————————————————————→

Recipe 21: Chicken Tikka Masala Spicy Curry With Rice and Naan Bread

SERVINGS: 4

PREPPING TIME: 15 MINUTES

COOK TIME: 30 MINUTES

DIFFICULTY: MEDIUM

Indulge in the aromatic flavors of Chicken Tikka Masala, a spicy curry infused with a medley of spices. This Instant Pot recipe ensures a quick yet delicious high-protein lunch paired perfectly with fluffy rice and soft naan bread.

Ingredients:

- ✓ 500g boneless chicken, cubed
- ✓ 2 cups basmati rice
- ✓ 2 large tomatoes, pureed
- ✓ 1 large onion, finely chopped
- ✓ 3 cloves garlic, minced
- ✓ 2 tsp ginger paste
- ✓ 2 tbsp yogurt
- ✓ 2 tsp garam masala
- ✓ 2 tsp turmeric powder
- ✓ 2 tsp red chili powder
- ✓ 1 tsp cumin seeds
- ✓ 3 tbsp oil
- ✓ 2 cups water
- ✓ Salt, to taste
- ✓ Fresh coriander leaves, for garnish
- ✓ 4 naan breads

Step-by-Step Preparation:

1. Start the Instant Pot on saute mode. Add oil and cumin seeds.
2. Once seeds splutter, add onions. Sauté till translucent.
3. Add garlic and ginger paste. Sauté for 2 minutes.
4. Stir in the pureed tomatoes, yogurt, and spices.
5. Add chicken cubes, ensuring they are well-coated with the masala.
6. Add water and stir.
7. Close the lid, and set the Instant Pot to 'Pressure Cook' mode for 20 minutes.
8. Release pressure, and garnish with coriander.
9. Serve hot with rice and naan bread.

Nutritional Facts: (Per serving)

- ❖ Calories: 560 kcal
- ❖ Protein: 40g
- ❖ Carbohydrates: 60g
- ❖ Dietary Fiber: 4g
- ❖ Fat: 20g
- ❖ Saturated Fat: 5g
- ❖ Sodium: 320mg
- ❖ Sugar: 5g

After a hectic morning, treat yourself to this heavenly chicken tikka masala dish. The fusion of spices mixed with tender chicken and paired with rice and naan bread provides a satisfying and flavorful experience, making your lunchtime truly special.

Recipe 22: Mung Dhal Palak With Green Spinach and Chapati

SERVINGS: 4

PREPPING TIME: 20 MINUTES

COOK TIME: 30 MINUTES

DIFFICULTY: EASY

Savor the delightful fusion of protein-packed mung dhal and nutrient-rich green spinach in this Instant Pot delicacy. This easy-to-make Mung Dhal Palak paired with chapati is mouth-watering and a wholesome treat for health enthusiasts.

Ingredients:

- ✓ 1 cup mung dhal, washed and soaked for 30 minutes
- ✓ 2 cups fresh green spinach, washed and chopped
- ✓ 3 chapatis, ready to serve
- ✓ 2 green chilies, finely chopped
- ✓ 1 teaspoon ginger, grated
- ✓ 2 cloves garlic, minced
- ✓ 1 onion, finely chopped
- ✓ 1 tomato, diced
- ✓ 1 teaspoon turmeric powder
- ✓ Salt, to taste
- ✓ 2 tablespoons oil or ghee
- ✓ 1 teaspoon cumin seeds

Step-by-Step Preparation:

1. Turn on the Instant Pot and set it to 'sauté' mode. Add oil or ghee.
2. Once hot, add cumin seeds, green chilies, ginger, and garlic. Sauté until aromatic.
3. Introduce the onions and sauté until translucent.
4. Add tomatoes, turmeric, and salt. Cook until tomatoes are soft.
5. Add the soaked mung dhal and 3 cups of water.
6. Close the Instant Pot lid and set it to 'pressure cook' for 15 minutes.
7. Quickly release the pressure, open the lid, and stir in the chopped spinach.
8. Set the Instant Pot to 'sauté' mode again and cook until the spinach is wilted.
9. Serve hot with chapati.

Nutritional Facts: (Per serving)

- ❖ Calories: 240
- ❖ Protein: 12g
- ❖ Carbohydrates: 38g
- ❖ Dietary Fiber: 7g
- ❖ Sugars: 3g
- ❖ Fat: 6g
- ❖ Saturated Fat: 1g
- ❖ Sodium: 280mg

Mung Dhal Palak with Chapati is a treat for the palate and the soul. Rich in proteins, fiber, and essential nutrients, this dish ensures a harmonious balance of taste and health. Dive into this traditional Indian delight and experience a whirlwind of flavors and wellness in every bite!

Recipe 23: Beef Goulash, Soup and a Stew

SERVINGS: 4

PREPPING TIME: 20 MINUTES

COOK TIME: 45 MINUTES

DIFFICULTY: INTERMEDIATE

Traditional Eastern European cuisine comes alive in this hearty, protein-packed goulash. Featuring tender beef chuck steak, robust potatoes, and the warm kick of paprika, it's a delightful union of soup and stew. Perfect for those seeking a filling, high-protein meal in an instant pot.

Ingredients:

- ✓ 1.5 lbs beef chuck steak, cubed
- ✓ 3 large potatoes, peeled and diced
- ✓ 2 tablespoons paprika
- ✓ 1 onion, finely chopped
- ✓ 3 cloves garlic, minced
- ✓ 4 cups beef broth
- ✓ 1 red bell pepper, diced
- ✓ 2 tablespoons tomato paste
- ✓ 2 teaspoons salt
- ✓ 1 teaspoon black pepper
- ✓ 2 tablespoons olive oil

Step-by-Step Preparation:

1. Set Instant Pot to 'Sauté' mode and heat olive oil.
2. Brown beef cubes until sealed, then remove.
3. Sauté onions and garlic until translucent.
4. Add paprika, stirring for 1 minute.
5. Return beef to the pot, and add potatoes, bell pepper, and tomato paste.
6. Pour in beef broth and season with salt and pepper.
7. Secure the Instant Pot lid and set it to 'Pressure Cook for 45 minutes.
8. Once cooked, allow to release naturally. Stir and serve.

Nutritional Facts: (Per serving)

- ❖ Calories: 380 kcal
- ❖ Protein: 28g
- ❖ Carbohydrates: 32g
- ❖ Dietary Fiber: 5g
- ❖ Fat: 16g
- ❖ Sodium: 890mg

When the calm winds blow, or you're craving a rich, protein-packed meal, this beef goulash promises a blend of flavors and warmth. Perfect for sharing or storing for future meals, this Instant Pot recipe offers a tasty adventure from Central Europe to your table.

Recipe 24: Rice With Fried Meat

SERVINGS: 4

PREPPING TIME: 15 MINUTES

COOK TIME: 20 MINUTES

DIFFICULTY: INTERMEDIATE

This delectable Rice With Fried Meat recipe satisfies your taste buds and protein needs. Crafted for instant pot lovers dish transforms staple ingredients into a wholesome, round-shaped serving that promises a gastronomic delight.

Ingredients:

- ✓ 2 cups of jasmine rice
- ✓ 500g lean meat (beef or chicken), sliced thinly
- ✓ 3 tbsp soy sauce
- ✓ 2 tbsp olive oil
- ✓ 1 medium onion, finely chopped
- ✓ 3 cloves garlic, minced
- ✓ 1 cup beef or chicken broth
- ✓ Salt and pepper, to taste
- ✓ Fresh coriander for garnish

Step-by-Step Preparation:

1. Turn the Instant Pot on "Sauté" mode. Add olive oil, chopped onion, and garlic. Sauté until translucent.

2. Add the thinly sliced meat. Fry until browned.

3. Pour in the soy sauce and stir.

4. Add the jasmine rice, then pour in the broth. Mix well.

5. Seal the Instant Pot and set it on "Rice" mode.

6. Once done, allow for a natural release.

7. Mold the rice and meat mixture into round shapes using a bowl or mold.

8. Garnish with fresh coriander before serving.

Nutritional Facts: (Per serving)

- ❖ Calories: 450
- ❖ Protein: 30g
- ❖ Carbohydrates: 40g
- ❖ Dietary Fiber: 2g
- ❖ Sugars: 1g
- ❖ Fat: 15g
- ❖ Saturated Fat: 5g
- ❖ Cholesterol: 75mg
- ❖ Sodium: 500mg

This Rice With Fried Meat served in a unique round shape, is a delightful merge of flavors and textures. Ideal for those on a high-protein diet or simply craving a hearty meal, this Instant Pot masterpiece will become a staple in your culinary repertoire. Bon appétit!

Recipe 25: Vegetarian Curry With Cauliflower and Chickpea

SERVINGS: 4

PREPPING TIME: 15 MINUTES

COOK TIME: 20 MINUTES

DIFFICULTY: INTERMEDIATE

Embrace the fusion of flavors with this Vegetarian Curry featuring cauliflower and chickpeas. An instant pot delicacy, this high-protein meal offers a nourishing, aromatic treat perfect for your lunchtime cravings.

Ingredients:

- ✓ 1 large cauliflower, cut into florets
- ✓ 1 can (15 oz) chickpeas, drained and rinsed
- ✓ 1 large onion, finely chopped
- ✓ 3 garlic cloves, minced
- ✓ 2 tbsp curry powder
- ✓ 1 can (14 oz) diced tomatoes
- ✓ 1 can (13.5 oz) coconut milk
- ✓ 2 tsp ginger, grated
- ✓ 1 tbsp olive oil
- ✓ Salt and pepper, to taste
- ✓ Fresh cilantro for garnish

Step-by-Step Preparation:

1. Set the instant pot to 'Sauté' mode and add olive oil.
2. Add onions and garlic, sautéing until translucent.
3. Mix in ginger and curry powder, stirring for 1 minute.
4. Incorporate cauliflower, chickpeas, tomatoes, and coconut milk. Season with salt and pepper.
5. Close the lid and set the instant pot to 'Pressure Cook' on high for 15 minutes.
6. Release pressure naturally for 5 minutes, then quick release.
7. Garnish with fresh cilantro before serving.

Nutritional Facts: (Per serving)

- ❖ Calories: 300
- ❖ Protein: 12g
- ❖ Carbohydrates: 34g
- ❖ Dietary Fiber: 9g
- ❖ Sugars: 8g
- ❖ Fat: 14g
- ❖ Saturated Fat: 9g
- ❖ Sodium: 420mg

Relish this Vegetarian Curry's creamy richness and depth with Cauliflower and Chickpeas. As an instant pot masterpiece, it promises convenience and a hearty, high-protein feast that will surely delight your palate and fuel your day.

Recipe 26: Lettuce Wraps Recipes

SERVINGS: 4

PREPPING TIME: 10 MINUTES

COOK TIME: 15 MINUTES

DIFFICULTY: EASY

Elevate your lunch game with these high-protein lettuce wraps. Packed with the perfect blend of savory meats, zesty sauces, and crispy veggies, they're nutritious and a delight to your taste buds. Using an Instant Pot ensures speedy preparation for those busy midday meals.

Ingredients:

- ✓ 4 large lettuce leaves (e.g., iceberg, romaine)
- ✓ 500g lean meat (chicken, beef, or pork)
- ✓ 2 tbsp soy sauce
- ✓ 1 tbsp sesame oil
- ✓ 1 bell pepper, sliced thinly
- ✓ 1 carrot, julienned
- ✓ 2 green onions, chopped
- ✓ 2 garlic cloves, minced
- ✓ 1 tbsp ginger, grated
- ✓ 2 tbsp hoisin sauce
- ✓ Optional toppings: crushed peanuts, fresh cilantro, or lime wedges

Step-by-Step Preparation:

1. Turn the Instant Pot to the sauté function. Add sesame oil, garlic, and ginger. Cook until fragrant.

2. Add your choice of lean meat and sauté until browned.

3. Pour in soy and hoisin sauces, mixing well.

4. Secure the lid and set the Instant Pot to pressure cook on high for 10 minutes.

5. Once done, allow for a natural release.

6. Prepare lettuce leaves on plates, spoon in the meat mixture, and top with veggies. Add optional toppings if desired.

Nutritional Facts: (Per serving)

- ❖ Calories: 250
- ❖ Protein: 30g
- ❖ Carbohydrates: 12g
- ❖ Dietary Fiber: 2g
- ❖ Sugars: 6g
- ❖ Fat: 9g
- ❖ Saturated Fat: 2g
- ❖ Sodium: 450mg

These high-protein lettuce wraps are perfect for a quick and healthy lunch. Combining the convenience of the Instant Pot with fresh, vibrant ingredients, you get a meal that's both delicious and beneficial for your health. They're so good you might find yourself making them again for dinner!

Recipe 27: Chicken Mushroom Risotto

SERVINGS: 4

PREPPING TIME: 15 MINUTES

COOK TIME: 20 MINUTES

DIFFICULTY: INTERMEDIATE

Indulge in the comforting flavors of Italy with this high-protein Chicken Mushroom Risotto. Perfectly cooked in an Instant Pot, this dish blends creamy risotto, succulent grilled chicken, and fresh mushrooms complemented by green beans tossed in rich Alfredo sauce. Ideal for a hearty lunch.

Ingredients:

- ✓ 1 cup Arborio rice
- ✓ 2 chicken breasts, grilled and sliced
- ✓ 200g fresh mushrooms, sliced
- ✓ 200g green beans, trimmed
- ✓ 1 cup Alfredo sauce
- ✓ 3 cups chicken broth
- ✓ 1 onion, finely chopped
- ✓ 2 cloves garlic, minced
- ✓ 2 tbsp olive oil
- ✓ Salt and pepper, to taste
- ✓ Grated Parmesan, for garnish
- ✓ Fresh parsley for garnish

Step-by-Step Preparation:

1. Set the Instant Pot to 'sauté' mode and heat olive oil.
2. Add onion and garlic, and sauté until translucent.
3. Stir in the mushrooms and cook for 2 minutes.
4. Add Arborio rice, ensuring grains are coated in oil.
5. Pour in chicken broth and season with salt and pepper.
6. Secure the lid, and set it to 'Pressure Cook' on high for 20 minutes.
7. Quickly release pressure and stir in grilled chicken slices.
8. In a separate pan, heat Alfredo sauce and toss with green beans.
9. Serve the risotto with green beans on the side, garnished with Parmesan and parsley.

Nutritional Facts: (Per serving)

- ❖ Calories: 520
- ❖ Protein: 35g
- ❖ Carbohydrates: 45g
- ❖ Fat: 20g
- ❖ Saturated Fat: 7g
- ❖ Fiber: 3g
- ❖ Sugar: 3g
- ❖ Sodium: 550mg

Indulging in this risotto's rich, creamy depths not only satiates your taste buds but also offers a protein-packed meal. The symphony of flavors and textures, from the tender chicken to the luscious Alfredo-coated beans, makes every bite a culinary delight. Pair with a crisp Italian salad for a balanced meal. Buon appetito!

Recipe 28: Moroccan Stew With Tender Chickpeas

SERVINGS: 4

PREPPING TIME: 15 MINUTES

COOK TIME: 26 MINUTES

DIFFICULTY: INTERMEDIATE

Dive into the aromatic realm of Moroccan cuisine with this Chickpeas Tagine. This savory stew combines tender chickpeas, aromatic spices, tomatoes, and onions, offering a protein-packed lunch option. Traditionally garnished with fresh herbs, it pairs perfectly with couscous or bread, elevating your mealtime experience.

Ingredients:

- ✓ 2 cups chickpeas, soaked overnight or canned
- ✓ 1 large onion, finely chopped
- ✓ 2 tomatoes, diced
- ✓ 3 garlic cloves, minced
- ✓ 1 tsp ground cumin
- ✓ 1 tsp ground coriander
- ✓ 1/2 tsp turmeric
- ✓ 1/2 tsp paprika
- ✓ Salt to taste
- ✓ 2 cups vegetable broth or water
- ✓ 2 tbsp olive oil
- ✓ Fresh herbs for garnish (cilantro or parsley)

Step-by-Step Preparation:

1. Turn the Instant Pot to sauté mode. Add olive oil and sauté onions until translucent.

2. Add garlic and spices, and stir for a minute until aromatic.

3. Incorporate the tomatoes and chickpeas, stirring well.

4. Pour in the vegetable broth or water and adjust the salt.

5. Close the Instant Pot lid, and set it to pressure cook on high for 20 minutes.

6. Once done, allow a natural release.

7. Garnish with fresh herbs before serving with couscous or bread.

Nutritional Facts: (Per serving)

- ❖ Calories: 280 kcal
- ❖ Protein: 12g
- ❖ Carbohydrates: 42g
- ❖ Fiber: 11g
- ❖ Fat: 7g
- ❖ Sodium: 320mg

Immerse yourself in a nourishing, flavorful journey with Chickpeas Tagine. Whether seeking a wholesome lunch or a comforting dinner, this Moroccan-inspired stew delivers nutrition and taste. Transport your senses and enjoy a delectable bite of tradition from the comfort of your home.

Recipe 29: Beef Barley Soup With Vegetables

SERVINGS: 4

PREPPING TIME: 20 MINUTES

COOK TIME: 35 MINUTES

DIFFICULTY: INTERMEDIATE

Warm up with this hearty Beef Barley Soup, brimming with savory beef, tender barley, and nutritious vegetables. Prepared in an Instant Pot, this protein-rich dish is perfect for a satisfying lunch on cold days.

Ingredients:

- ✓ 1 lb beef chunks
- ✓ ½ cup barley
- ✓ 2 tomatoes, diced
- ✓ 1 potato, diced
- ✓ ½ cup green peas
- ✓ 1 carrot, sliced

- ✓ 2 celery stalks, chopped
- ✓ 1 onion, finely chopped
- ✓ 4 cups beef broth
- ✓ 2 slices of bread for serving
- ✓ Salt and pepper to taste

Step-by-Step Preparation:

1. Turn the Instant Pot to sauté mode. Add beef chunks and brown on all sides.
2. Add onion and sauté until translucent.
3. Stir in tomatoes, potatoes, green peas, carrots, and celery.
4. Pour in beef broth and add barley.
5. Season with salt and pepper.
6. Close the lid and set the Instant Pot to "Pressure Cook" for 30 minutes.
7. Allow for natural release, then stir well.
8. Serve hot, accompanied with slices of bread.

Nutritional Facts: (Per serving)

- ❖ Calories: 450
- ❖ Protein: 30g
- ❖ Carbohydrates: 50g
- ❖ Dietary Fiber: 10g

- ❖ Sugars: 5g
- ❖ Fat: 15g
- ❖ Saturated Fat: 5g
- ❖ Sodium: 800mg

This Beef Barley Soup is a harmonious blend of savory flavors and wholesome nutrition. Perfect for those chilly days when you crave warmth and nourishment, this Instant Pot masterpiece will fill your belly and fuel your body with high-quality protein. Please don't skip the bread; it adds the perfect finishing touch!

Recipe 30: Stir Fried Long Beans Mixed With Tempeh

SERVINGS: 4

PREPPING TIME: 10 MINUTES

COOK TIME: 15 MINUTES

DIFFICULTY: EASY

Stir-Fried Long Beans Mixed with Tempeh is a delectable, protein-packed lunch dish, perfect for those on the go. With the magic of the Instant Pot, you'll bring the rich flavors of this Asian-inspired recipe to life in record time.

Ingredients:

- ✓ 200g tempeh, cubed
- ✓ 300g long beans, cut into 2-inch lengths
- ✓ 3 tablespoons soy sauce
- ✓ 2 tablespoons sesame oil
- ✓ 3 cloves garlic, minced
- ✓ 1 red chili, thinly sliced (optional)
- ✓ 2 tablespoons vegetable oil
- ✓ 1 tablespoon toasted sesame seeds (for garnish)
- ✓ Salt and pepper to taste

Step-by-Step Preparation:

1. Set the Instant Pot to sauté mode. Add the vegetable oil and heat.
2. Add garlic and chili (if using), and sauté until fragrant.
3. Add tempeh cubes and stir-fry until lightly browned.
4. Add long beans, soy sauce, and sesame oil. Mix well.
5. Close the Instant Pot lid and set it to pressure cook for 5 minutes.
6. Once cooked, release the pressure and open the lid.
7. Adjust seasoning with salt and pepper. Transfer to a serving dish and garnish with toasted sesame seeds.

Nutritional Facts: (Per serving)

- ❖ **Calories:** 220
- ❖ **Protein:** 14g
- ❖ **Carbohydrates:** 15g
- ❖ **Dietary Fiber:** 5g
- ❖ **Fat:** 12g
- ❖ **Saturated Fat:** 2g
- ❖ **Sodium:** 480mg

There you have it - a protein-rich, delicious meal that'll fill you up without weighing you down. Combining crispy tempeh and tender long beans in the Stir-Fried Long Beans Mixed with Tempeh dish ensures a satisfying bite every time. Perfect for those in search of a quick, healthy lunch option!

Recipe 31: Roasted Garlic and Rosemary White Bean Dip

SERVINGS: 4

PREPPING TIME: 15 MINUTES

COOK TIME: 30 MINUTES

DIFFICULTY: MEDIUM

Delight your taste buds with this creamy and flavorful dip, crafted using cannellini beans and enriched with the aromatic blend of roasted garlic and rosemary. This high-protein afternoon snack whipped up effortlessly in an Instant Pot, is perfect to pair with crispy pita chips.

Ingredients:

- ✓ 1 can (15 oz) cannellini beans, rinsed and drained
- ✓ 6 cloves of roasted garlic
- ✓ 2 tablespoons olive oil
- ✓ 1 tablespoon fresh rosemary, finely chopped
- ✓ Salt and pepper to taste
- ✓ 2 tablespoons water (or as needed)
- ✓ Pita chips for serving

Step-by-Step Preparation:

1. Place cannellini beans, roasted garlic, olive oil, and rosemary into the Instant Pot.
2. Blend until smooth, adding water if necessary to achieve desired consistency.
3. Season with salt and pepper to taste.
4. If desired, transfer to a serving bowl and drizzle with more olive oil.
5. Serve immediately with pita chips.

Nutritional Facts: (Per serving)

- ❖ Calories: 140
- ❖ Protein: 7g
- ❖ Carbohydrates: 18g
- ❖ Dietary Fiber: 5g
- ❖ Sugars: 1g
- ❖ Fat: 6g
- ❖ Saturated Fat: 1g
- ❖ Sodium: 300mg

Indulge in a snack that's not only delectable but also nutritious. The Roasted Garlic and Rosemary White Bean Dip combines classic Mediterranean ingredients' rustic essence in an easy-to-make recipe. It's a great addition to your recipe collection, ideal for health-conscious gourmets. Enjoy it at your next get-together or a simple afternoon indulgence!

Recipe 32: Buffalo Chicken Dip Served With Chips and Fresh Vegetables

SERVINGS: 6

PREPPING TIME: 15 MINUTES

COOK TIME: 20 MINUTES

DIFFICULTY: INTERMEDIATE

Dive into the rich, savory layers of this Buffalo Chicken Dip, an instant pot creation that is a must-try. The perfect high-protein afternoon snack pairs well with chips and fresh vegetables, offering flavors and textures to delight the senses.

Ingredients:

- ✓ 2 cups shredded chicken (cooked)
- ✓ 1 cup buffalo wing sauce
- ✓ 1 cup cream cheese, softened
- ✓ 1/2 cup ranch dressing
- ✓ 1/2 cup crumbled blue cheese
- ✓ 1 cup shredded cheddar cheese
- ✓ 1 tbsp chopped fresh parsley
- ✓ Tortilla chips for serving
- ✓ Assorted fresh vegetables (like celery and carrot sticks) for serving

Step-by-Step Preparation:

1. Turn the Instant Pot on sauté mode and mix in cream cheese, ranch dressing, and buffalo sauce until well blended.
2. Stir in shredded chicken and blue cheese.
3. Secure the lid and set the Instant Pot to manual high pressure for 10 minutes.
4. Once cooked, release the pressure and stir well.
5. Transfer to a serving dish and sprinkle with cheddar cheese and parsley.
6. Serve warm with tortilla chips and fresh vegetables.

Nutritional Facts: (Per serving)

- ❖ Calories: 280
- ❖ Protein: 18g
- ❖ Carbohydrates: 5g
- ❖ Dietary Fiber: 1g
- ❖ Sugars: 2g
- ❖ Fat: 22g
- ❖ Saturated Fat: 9g
- ❖ Cholesterol: 65mg
- ❖ Sodium: 890mg

This Buffalo Chicken Dip promises an irresistible taste experience. The balance of creamy cheese, spicy buffalo sauce, and tender chicken is pure perfection. The added benefit of being high-protein makes for a wholesome treat. Enjoy it during an afternoon get-together or a simple snack break, and let the flavors whisk you away.

Recipe 33: Red Lentil Pate With Nuts, Carrots and Oats

SERVINGS: 4

PREPPING TIME: 10 MINUTES

COOK TIME: 15 MINUTES

DIFFICULTY: EASY

Red Lentil Pate is a delicious, nutritious afternoon snack with protein and flavors. Using an Instant Pot, this dish comes together quickly, making it a perfect pick-me-up during your day.

Ingredients:

- ✓ 1 cup red lentils, washed and drained
- ✓ 2 medium carrots, grated
- ✓ 1/2 cup mixed nuts (walnuts, almonds, cashews)
- ✓ 1/2 cup rolled oats
- ✓ 2 tbsp olive oil
- ✓ 2 garlic cloves, minced
- ✓ Salt and pepper, to taste
- ✓ 1 tsp paprika
- ✓ 1/4 cup fresh parsley, chopped

Step-by-Step Preparation:

1. Place all ingredients, except parsley, into the Instant Pot.
2. Seal and set to Manual mode for 15 minutes.
3. Once cooked, release the pressure and open the pot.
4. Blend the mixture until smooth using a hand blender.
5. Stir in the fresh parsley.
6. Let it cool and serve with crackers or fresh veggies.

Nutritional Facts: (Per serving)

- ❖ Calories: 220
- ❖ Protein: 13g
- ❖ Carbs: 30g
- ❖ Fiber: 8g
- ❖ Sugars: 2g
- ❖ Fat: 7g
- ❖ Sodium: 80mg

This Red Lentil Pate with Nuts, Carrots, and Oats is a delightful fusion of flavors and textures. Ideal as an energy-boosting afternoon snack, its high protein content ensures you'll feel satiated and fueled until dinner. Enjoy the hearty taste and health benefits of this versatile pate.

Recipe 34: Pizza With Ham and Mozzarella

SERVINGS: 4

PREPPING TIME: 10 MINUTES

COOK TIME: 20 MINUTES

DIFFICULTY: EASY

Warm, cheesy, and delightful, this Pizza with Ham and Mozzarella is the perfect high-protein snack for any afternoon. Prepared using an Instant Pot, it guarantees deliciousness and ensures a hassle-free cooking experience.

Ingredients:

- ✓ 1 pizza dough (store-bought or homemade)
- ✓ 1 cup pizza sauce
- ✓ 1 cup mozzarella cheese, shredded
- ✓ 8 slices of ham, thinly sliced
- ✓ 1 tsp dried oregano
- ✓ 1/2 tsp red pepper flakes (optional)
- ✓ Fresh basil leaves for garnishing

Step-by-Step Preparation:

1. Roll out the pizza dough on a floured surface.
2. Place the rolled-out dough in the Instant Pot.
3. Spread the pizza sauce evenly over the dough.
4. Top with mozzarella cheese and ham slices.
5. Sprinkle with oregano and red pepper flakes.
6. Set the Instant Pot to 'Bake' mode and cook for 20 minutes.
7. Once done, garnish with fresh basil leaves before serving.

Nutritional Facts: (Per serving)

- ❖ Calories: 250
- ❖ Protein: 18g
- ❖ Fat: 8g
- ❖ Carbohydrates: 28g
- ❖ Fiber: 2g
- ❖ Sugar: 4g

There you have it – a high-protein, mouth-watering pizza snack that is nutritious and delectable. Perfect for those afternoons when you crave something savory, this Pizza with Ham and Mozzarella will quickly become a favorite in your household. Enjoy it with a side salad or on its own – it's sheer delight!

Recipe 35: Chicken Meatballs in Coconut Curry Sauce

SERVINGS: 4

PREPPING TIME: 20 MINUTES

COOK TIME: 15 MINUTES

DIFFICULTY: MEDIUM

Indulge in the rich flavors of chicken meatballs simmered in a creamy coconut curry sauce topped with fresh cilantro. This high-protein Instant Pot snack is perfect for your afternoon hunger pangs, ensuring taste and health in one bowl.

Ingredients:

- ✓ 500g ground chicken
- ✓ 1 cup breadcrumbs
- ✓ 1 egg
- ✓ 2 tsp ginger-garlic paste
- ✓ 1 can (400ml) coconut milk
- ✓ 2 tbsp red curry paste
- ✓ 1/2 cup chopped cilantro
- ✓ Salt to taste
- ✓ 1 tbsp olive oil
- ✓ 1 tsp ground turmeric

Step-by-Step Preparation:

1. Mix ground chicken, breadcrumbs, egg, ginger-garlic paste, and salt in a bowl.
2. Form into small meatballs and set aside.
3. Turn on the Instant Pot to sauté mode. Add olive oil.
4. Brown the meatballs on all sides.
5. Add red curry paste, coconut milk, and turmeric. Stir well.
6. Close the Instant Pot lid and pressure cook for 10 minutes.
7. Release pressure naturally and stir in chopped cilantro.

Nutritional Facts: (Per serving)

- ❖ Calories: 380
- ❖ Protein: 25g
- ❖ Carbohydrates: 20g
- ❖ Fats: 22g
- ❖ Fiber: 2g
- ❖ Sugars: 4g

Elevate your snack time with this delightful blend of succulent chicken and aromatic coconut curry. Topped with fresh cilantro meatballs promises a culinary journey, making your afternoon breaks more exciting and nourishing. Perfect for those seeking a protein-packed, mouth-watering treat!

Recipe 36: Hummus With Avocado and Beans Edamame

SERVINGS: 4

PREPPING TIME: 15 MINUTES

COOK TIME: 10 MINUTES

DIFFICULTY: EASY

Indulge in a delectable fusion of flavors with this high-protein Hummus topped with avocado and edamame beans. An Instant Pot snack is perfect for a nutrient-packed afternoon treat, paired with crisp corn tortillas and fresh vegetables.

Ingredients:

- ✓ 1 can chickpeas, drained and rinsed
- ✓ 1 ripe avocado, peeled and pitted
- ✓ 1 cup edamame beans, shelled
- ✓ 2 cloves garlic, minced
- ✓ 2 tbsp tahini
- ✓ Juice of 1 lemon
- ✓ 3 tbsp olive oil
- ✓ Salt, to taste
- ✓ Fresh vegetables (e.g., cucumber, bell peppers) for serving
- ✓ Corn tortilla crisps for serving

Step-by-Step Preparation:

1. In the Instant Pot, steam edamame beans for 5 minutes.
2. In a food processor, combine chickpeas, steamed edamame, garlic, tahini, lemon juice, and olive oil.
3. Blend until smooth.
4. Add avocado and pulse until combined.
5. Season with salt to taste.
6. Transfer to a bowl and serve with sliced fresh vegetables and corn tortilla crisps.

Nutritional Facts: (Per serving)

- ❖ Calories: 250
- ❖ Protein: 9g
- ❖ Carbohydrates: 20g
- ❖ Dietary Fiber: 7g
- ❖ Sugars: 2g
- ❖ Fat: 16g
- ❖ Saturated Fat: 2.5g
- ❖ Sodium: 150mg

Elevate your snack game with this protein-packed Hummus. The creamy texture of avocado and the goodness of edamame beans make for a delightful treat. Paired with the crunch of corn tortilla and fresh veggies, it's the ideal healthy snack for any afternoon craving. Enjoy and relish every bite

Recipe 37: Grilled Buffalo Chicken Sandwich

SERVINGS: 4

PREPPING TIME: 15 MINUTES

COOK TIME: 20 MINUTES

DIFFICULTY: EASY

Delight your taste buds with a high-protein Grilled Buffalo Chicken Sandwich Wrap, perfect for those seeking a filling yet delectable afternoon snack. Combined with the tang of bleu cheese and the crunch of romaine lettuce recipe is an instant pot marvel.

Ingredients:

- ✓ 2 boneless chicken breasts
- ✓ 1/2 cup buffalo sauce
- ✓ 4 large tortilla wraps
- ✓ 1 cup romaine lettuce, chopped
- ✓ 1/2 cup bleu cheese crumbles
- ✓ 1 cup fries, cooked
- ✓ 2 tbsp olive oil
- ✓ Salt and pepper, to taste

Step-by-Step Preparation:

1. Season chicken with salt and pepper, and drizzle with olive oil.
2. Place chicken in the Instant Pot and set to "Sauté" mode until lightly browned on both sides.
3. Pour buffalo sauce over the chicken and set the Instant Pot to "Manual" mode for 10 minutes.
4. Once cooked, shred the chicken inside the pot, mixing it with the sauce.
5. Lay out tortilla wraps, add shredded buffalo chicken, sprinkle bleu cheese and lettuce, and top with fries.
6. Roll the wraps tightly and serve immediately.

Nutritional Facts: (Per serving)

- ❖ Calories: 410
- ❖ Protein: 28g
- ❖ Carbs: 32g
- ❖ Fats: 18g
- ❖ Sodium: 950mg
- ❖ Sugars: 3g

Experience an explosion of flavors and textures with this Grilled Buffalo Chicken Sandwich Wrap. It's a protein-packed treat to satiate your hunger, while the bleu cheese and buffalo sauce combo entices your palate. Elevate your afternoon snacks and relish the delectable simplicity of this dish. Enjoy!

Recipe 38: Chickpea Salad With Vegetables

SERVINGS: 4

PREPPING TIME: 15 MINUTES

COOK TIME: 20 MINUTES

DIFFICULTY: EASY

A refreshing burst of flavors awaits with this Chickpea Salad, combining the crunch of fresh veggies with the protein-packed goodness of chickpeas. Perfect for those following a high-protein diet, this Instant Pot recipe ensures a speedy and delightful afternoon treat.

Ingredients:

- ✓ 1 cup dried chickpeas, soaked overnight
- ✓ 2 large tomatoes, diced
- ✓ 1 cucumber, diced
- ✓ 1/2 cup feta cheese, crumbled
- ✓ 1/4 cup fresh parsley, chopped
- ✓ 1 medium onion, finely sliced
- ✓ Juice of 1 lemon
- ✓ Salt and pepper to taste
- ✓ 2 cups water (for Instant Pot)

Step-by-Step Preparation:

1. Place soaked chickpeas and water in the Instant Pot.
2. Secure the lid and set to Pressure Cook on high for 15 minutes.
3. Once done, quickly release the pressure and drain the chickpeas.
4. Mix the cooked chickpeas with tomatoes, cucumber, feta cheese, parsley, and onions in a large bowl.
5. Drizzle with lemon juice, and season with salt and pepper. Toss well.

Nutritional Facts: (Per serving)

- ❖ Calories: 220
- ❖ Protein: 11g
- ❖ Carbohydrates: 29g
- ❖ Fiber: 7g
- ❖ Fat: 7g
- ❖ Sugars: 5g
- ❖ Sodium: 280mg

Revel in the crunchy veggies, creamy feta, and wholesome chickpeas, making this salad the ultimate afternoon pick-me-up. Whether fueling a workout or simply seeking a satisfying, protein-packed snack, this Chickpea Salad promises to be your go-to, easy-to-whip delight. Cheers to a healthier afternoon!

Recipe 39: White Bean and Tuna Salad

SERVINGS: 4

PREPPING TIME: 10 MINUTES

COOK TIME: 20 MINUTES

DIFFICULTY: EASY

A delightful fusion of flavors and nutrients, this White Bean and Tuna Salad, is your go-to High Protein Instant Pot snack. Perfect for those afternoons when you crave something nutritious yet quick to prepare, this dish will become a regular in your healthy snack rotation.

Ingredients:

- ✓ 2 cans (15 oz each) of white beans, drained and rinsed
- ✓ 1 can (5 oz) tuna in water, drained
- ✓ 1/4 cup chopped fresh parsley
- ✓ 2 tbsp olive oil
- ✓ 1 lemon, juiced
- ✓ Salt and pepper to taste
- ✓ 1/4 cup red onion, finely diced
- ✓ 1/2 cup cherry tomatoes, halved

Step-by-Step Preparation:

1. Add white beans and a cup of water to the Instant Pot. Close the lid and set to pressure cook on high for 20 minutes.

2. Once done, release the pressure and open the lid. Drain any excess water.

3. Transfer beans to a mixing bowl.

4. Add tuna, parsley, olive oil, lemon juice, salt, pepper, red onion, and cherry tomatoes.

5. Toss gently until everything is well combined.

6. Chill in the refrigerator for at least 30 minutes before serving.

Nutritional Facts: (Per serving)

- ❖ Calories: 220
- ❖ Protein: 18g
- ❖ Carbohydrates: 28g
- ❖ Dietary Fiber: 6g
- ❖ Fat: 5g
- ❖ Sodium: 320mg

Indulge in this refreshing White Bean and Tuna Salad, where every bite offers a flavor and a protein punch. Not only is it a delightful snack, but it also holds its own as a light lunch or dinner. With the Instant Pot's convenience and its ingredients' wholesomeness, this dish promises to be both tasty and healthy.

Recipe 40: Pulled Pork Nachos

SERVINGS: 4

PREPPING TIME: 15 MINUTES

COOK TIME: 60 MINUTES

DIFFICULTY: MODERATE

Indulge in these savory pulled pork nachos. A delightful treat, they combine the succulence of perfectly cooked pork with the crunch of nachos, ensuring an unforgettable snack experience.

Ingredients:

- ✓ 1 lb pulled pork
- ✓ 1 bag tortilla chips (approx. 200g)
- ✓ 1 cup shredded cheddar cheese
- ✓ 1/2 cup diced tomatoes
- ✓ 1/4 cup sliced jalapeños
- ✓ 1/4 cup diced red onions
- ✓ 1/4 cup chopped cilantro
- ✓ 2 tbsp olive oil
- ✓ Sour cream for serving (optional)

Step-by-Step Preparation:

1. Start by placing the pulled pork in the Instant Pot with olive oil. Cook on the 'Meat/Stew' setting for 60 minutes.

2. Once done, allow a natural release for 10 minutes.

3. Preheat oven to 375°F (190°C).

4. Spread tortilla chips on a baking tray.

5. Evenly distribute the pulled pork over the chips.

6. Sprinkle with cheddar cheese, diced tomatoes, jalapeños, and red onions.

7. Bake in the oven for 10-12 minutes or until cheese is melted and bubbly.

8. Remove from oven and sprinkle with fresh cilantro.

9. Serve hot with sour cream on the side.

Nutritional Facts: (Per serving)

- ❖ Calories: 550
- ❖ Protein: 28g
- ❖ Carbohydrates: 38g
- ❖ Dietary Fiber: 3g
- ❖ Sugars: 2g
- ❖ Fat: 30g
- ❖ Sodium: 650mg

Savor the fusion of tender pork and crispy nachos in this flavorful dish. Perfect for afternoon cravings, this high-protein snack is delicious and fulfilling. Please share with friends or enjoy solo; either way, it's bound to be a favorite!

← →

Recipe 41: Lemon and Herb Whole Chicken

SERVINGS: 4

PREPPING TIME: 20 MINUTES

COOK TIME: 45 MINUTES

DIFFICULTY: MODERATE

Elevate your dinner game with this Lemon and Herb Whole Chicken cooked to perfection in an Instant Pot. Infused with fragrant herbs and tangy lemon, it's a high-protein meal that's healthy and delicious.

Ingredients:

- ✓ 1 whole chicken (about 4-5 lbs.)
- ✓ 2 lemons, zested and juiced
- ✓ 3 garlic cloves, minced
- ✓ 1 tablespoon fresh rosemary, chopped
- ✓ 1 tablespoon fresh thyme, chopped
- ✓ 2 tablespoons olive oil
- ✓ Salt and pepper to taste

Step-by-Step Preparation:

1. Clean the chicken, remove the giblets, and pat dry with paper towels.
2. Combine lemon zest, lemon juice, garlic, rosemary, thyme, olive oil, salt, and pepper in a bowl.
3. Rub the mixture all over the chicken, ensuring it's well-coated.
4. Place the chicken in the Instant Pot.
5. Set the Instant Pot to "Poultry" and cook for 45 minutes.
6. Once done, let the pressure release naturally for 10 minutes.
7. Carefully remove the chicken from the Instant Pot and let it rest for a few minutes before carving.

Nutritional Facts: (Per serving)

- ❖ Calories: 380
- ❖ Protein: 35g
- ❖ Fat: 24g
- ❖ Carbohydrates: 2g
- ❖ Fiber: 0.5g
- ❖ Sugars: 1g

Enjoy the juiciness and flavor of Lemon and Herb Whole Chicken from your Instant Pot, providing a comforting and protein-rich dinner option. Serve with your favorite sides, and let the compliments roll in. The fusion of lemon and herbs tantalizes your taste buds and ensures a nutritious feast.

Recipe 42: Mushroom Beef Stroganoff

SERVINGS: 4

PREPPING TIME: 15 MINUTES

COOK TIME: 30 MINUTES

DIFFICULTY: INTERMEDIATE

Indulge in the rich and savory taste of this Mushroom Beef Stroganoff. Made in an Instant Pot, this high-protein dinner boasts a harmonious blend of cremini and champignon mushrooms, elevating the classic stroganoff to new heights.

Ingredients:

- ✓ 1 lb beef strips
- ✓ 1 cup sliced cremini mushrooms
- ✓ 1 cup sliced champignon mushrooms
- ✓ 1 onion, finely chopped
- ✓ 2 garlic cloves, minced
- ✓ 2 cups beef broth
- ✓ 1 cup sour cream

- ✓ 2 tbsp olive oil
- ✓ 2 tbsp all-purpose flour
- ✓ 1 tsp paprika
- ✓ Salt and pepper to taste
- ✓ Chopped parsley for garnish
- ✓ 12 oz egg noodles

Step-by-Step Preparation:

1. Set the Instant Pot to 'Sauté' mode and heat olive oil.
2. Add beef strips, seasoning with salt, pepper, and paprika. Sauté until browned.
3. Remove beef and add onion, garlic, and both mushroom types. Sauté until softened.
4. Return the beef to the pot and sprinkle flour over it. Mix.
5. Pour in beef broth, stir, and seal the pot.
6. Set Instant Pot to 'Pressure Cook' for 20 minutes.
7. Release pressure naturally, open the lid, and stir in sour cream.
8. Serve hot cooked egg noodles garnished with parsley.

Nutritional Facts: (Per serving)

- ❖ Calories: 500
- ❖ Protein: 28g
- ❖ Carbohydrates: 46g
- ❖ Fat: 20g
- ❖ Sodium: 600mg
- ❖ Fiber: 3g

Whether you want to build muscle or enjoy a hearty meal after a long day, this Mushroom Beef Stroganoff will surely hit the spot. With the convenience of an Instant Pot, this dish is protein-packed and a timesaver, proving that gourmet can indeed be easy. Enjoy with a side salad for a complete meal!

Recipe 43: Vegan Curry With Cauliflower

SERVINGS: 4

PREPPING TIME: 20 MINUTES

COOK TIME: 30 MINUTES

DIFFICULTY: MEDIUM

Dive into a pot of aromatic flavors with this Vegan Curry. Bursting with the goodness of cauliflower, chickpeas, and butternut squash and topped with crunchy peanuts Instant Pot dish is a protein-packed delight, perfectly complemented by a side of rice and fresh cilantro.

Ingredients:

- ✓ 1 medium cauliflower, cut into florets
- ✓ 1 can chickpeas, drained and rinsed
- ✓ 1 small butternut squash, peeled and diced
- ✓ 1/2 cup unsalted peanuts
- ✓ 2 cups cooked rice
- ✓ 2 tablespoons curry powder

- ✓ 1 can of coconut milk
- ✓ 2 tablespoons olive oil
- ✓ 1 onion, finely chopped
- ✓ 3 cloves garlic, minced
- ✓ Salt and pepper to taste
- ✓ Fresh cilantro for garnish

Step-by-Step Preparation:

1. Set Instant Pot to 'sauté' mode and heat olive oil.
2. Add onions and garlic, sautéing until translucent.
3. Add curry powder and stir for a minute until fragrant.
4. Incorporate cauliflower, chickpeas, and butternut squash.
5. Pour in the coconut milk, ensuring all ingredients are submerged. Season with salt and pepper.
6. Secure the lid and set it to 'manual' or 'pressure cook' for 25 minutes.
7. Quickly release the pressure and open the lid.
8. Stir well, and serve over rice, garnished with peanuts and fresh cilantro.

Nutritional Facts (Per serving)

- ❖ Calories: 520
- ❖ Protein: 18g
- ❖ Carbohydrates: 75g
- ❖ Dietary Fiber: 15g

- ❖ Sugars: 8g
- ❖ Fat: 20g
- ❖ Saturated Fat: 9g
- ❖ Sodium: 120mg

Warm, hearty, and beautifully spiced, this vegan curry promises taste and wholesome nutrition. The high-protein ingredients make it ideal for active lifestyles, while the Instant Pot ensures a fuss-free cooking experience. Recharge your evenings with this plateful of comfort, and enjoy the medley of flavors and textures.

Recipe 44: Spicy Cajun Jambalaya Packed With Sausage, Shrimp and Chicken

SERVINGS: 6

PREPPING TIME: 20 MINUTES

COOK TIME: 25 MINUTES

DIFFICULTY: MEDIUM

Dive into the heart of Louisiana with this high-protein Instant Pot dinner. A seamless blend of sausage, shrimp, and chicken, this spicy Cajun jambalaya promises a flavor-packed meal that warms your soul.

Ingredients:

✓ 1 lb smoked sausage, sliced

✓ 1 lb chicken breast, diced

✓ 1 lb raw shrimp, peeled and deveined

✓ 1 onion, finely chopped

✓ 2 bell peppers, diced

✓ 3 cloves garlic, minced

✓ 1 ½ cups long-grain rice

✓ 1 can (14 oz) diced tomatoes, undrained

✓ 2 ½ cups chicken broth

✓ 2 tsp Cajun seasoning

✓ 2 bay leaves

✓ Salt and pepper to taste

✓ 2 tbsp olive oil

✓ Chopped green onions and parsley for garnish

Step-by-Step Preparation:

1. Set Instant Pot to Sauté mode and heat oil.

2. Brown sausage and chicken pieces until lightly golden.

3. Add onions, bell peppers, and garlic, sautéing until translucent.

4. Stir in rice, tomatoes, Cajun seasoning, bay leaves, salt, and pepper.

5. Pour in chicken broth and mix well.

6. Close the lid, and set it to Pressure Cook on High for 8 minutes.

7. Quickly release pressure, add shrimp, and cook on Sauté until they turn pink.

8. Garnish with green onions and parsley.

Nutritional Facts: (Per serving)

❖ Calories: 510

❖ Protein: 35g

❖ Carbohydrates: 40g

❖ Fats: 20g

❖ Dietary Fiber: 2g

❖ Sodium: 800mg

Savor the rich tapestry of flavors that this Cajun Jambalaya brings to your plate. Perfect for those seeking a protein-packed dinner with a hint of Southern flair, this Instant Pot recipe will have everyone asking for seconds. Enjoy a side of crusty bread or a fresh salad for a complete meal.

Recipe 45: Juicy Baked Pork Tenderloin in Honey-Garlic Sauce

SERVINGS: 4

PREPPING TIME: 15 MINUTES

COOK TIME: 30 MINUTES

DIFFICULTY: EASY

Succulent and flavorful, this juicy baked pork tenderloin glazed with honey-garlic sauce is a high-protein treat. Made effortlessly in the Instant Pot and paired with fresh veggies, it's perfect for those seeking nutrition without compromising taste.

Ingredients:

- ✓ 1 pork tenderloin (about 1.5 lbs)
- ✓ 4 cloves garlic, minced
- ✓ 1/4 cup honey
- ✓ 2 tablespoons soy sauce
- ✓ 1 tablespoon olive oil
- ✓ 1 teaspoon dried rosemary (or fresh)
- ✓ Salt and pepper to taste
- ✓ 1 cup fresh vegetables (e.g., bell peppers, zucchini, broccoli)

Step-by-Step Preparation:

1. Mix honey, minced garlic, soy sauce, rosemary, salt, and pepper in a bowl.
2. Rub the pork tenderloin with the prepared sauce.
3. Set the Instant Pot to sauté mode and add olive oil. Brown the pork on all sides.
4. Close the Instant Pot lid and set it to manual pressure for 20 minutes.
5. Quickly release the pressure and remove the lid. Add the fresh vegetables.
6. Set the Instant Pot to sauté mode again and cook until vegetables are tender.
7. Serve the pork sliced, drizzled with any remaining sauce, and accompanied by the sautéed vegetables.

Nutritional Facts: (Per serving)

- ❖ Calories: 320
- ❖ Protein: 28g
- ❖ Carbs: 22g
- ❖ Fats: 12g
- ❖ Fiber: 2g
- ❖ Sugars: 18g

Indulge in a dinner that satiates both your palate and your health goals. This honey-garlic glazed pork tenderloin paired with vibrant veggies promises a flavorful journey with every bite. Ideal for busy nights or when you need a touch of gourmet at home, this Instant Pot recipe is sure to become a favorite.

Recipe 46: Lasagna With Meat and Spinach

SERVINGS: 6

PREPPING TIME: 20 MINUTES

COOK TIME: 30 MINUTES

DIFFICULTY: MODERATE

Dive into the layers of our Lasagna With Meat and Spinach, an ideal high-protein dish that combines the richness of meat with the freshness of spinach. Prepared in an Instant Pot, this dinner is both delicious and time-efficient.

Ingredients:

- 12 lasagna noodles
- 1 lb ground beef or turkey
- 2 cups fresh spinach, chopped
- 2 cups ricotta cheese
- 1 cup grated mozzarella cheese
- 1/2 cup grated Parmesan cheese
- 2.5 cups marinara sauce
- 1 onion, chopped
- 2 garlic cloves, minced
- 2 tsp olive oil
- Salt and pepper to taste
- 1 tsp dried oregano
- 1 tsp dried basil

Step-by-Step Preparation:

1. Turn on the Instant Pot to sauté mode and heat the olive oil. Add onions and garlic, cooking until translucent.

2. Add the ground meat, salt, and pepper. Cook until browned.

3. Stir in the marinara sauce, dried oregano, and basil.

4. Lay a few lasagna noodles at the bottom of the pot, then layer with the meat mixture, ricotta, spinach, and mozzarella. Repeat layers until all ingredients are used.

5. Secure the Instant Pot lid set to manual pressure for 20 minutes. Once done, allow a natural release for 10 minutes.

6. Sprinkle with Parmesan cheese before serving.

Nutritional Facts: (Per serving)

- Calories: 510
- Protein: 35g
- Carbohydrates: 42g
- Fat: 22g
- Fiber: 3g
- Sugar: 6g
- Sodium: 570mg

Lasagna With Meat and Spinach offers the best of both worlds: indulgence and nutrition. The Instant Pot makes the process seamless, letting you enjoy a gourmet meal without the extended wait. Each bite is a fusion of creamy ricotta, hearty meat, and leafy spinach, ensuring you relish a satiating and savory dinner.

Recipe 47: Pasta Fettuccine Alfredo and Penne With Tomato Sauce

SERVINGS: 2

PREPPING TIME: 15 MINUTES

COOK TIME: 12 MINUTES

DIFFICULTY: EASY

Indulge in Italy's rich, creamy flavors with this duo of pasta dishes: fettuccine alfredo and penne with tomato sauce. Prepared effortlessly in your Instant Pot, this high-protein dinner will surely be a favorite.

Ingredients:

- ✓ 1 cup fettuccine pasta
- ✓ 1 cup penne pasta
- ✓ 1/2 cup heavy cream
- ✓ 1/2 cup grated parmesan cheese
- ✓ 1 tablespoon olive oil

- ✓ 1 cup tomato sauce
- ✓ 2 garlic cloves, minced
- ✓ 1/2 cup diced chicken breast
- ✓ Salt and pepper, to taste
- ✓ Fresh basil and parsley for garnish

Step-by-Step Preparation:

1. Combine penne, tomato sauce, garlic, chicken, olive oil, salt, and pepper in the Instant Pot.
2. Cook on manual high pressure for 6 minutes.
3. Quickly release the pressure and remove the penne mixture. Keep it warm.
4. Add fettuccine, heavy cream, and parmesan cheese, and season with salt and pepper in the same pot.
5. Cook on manual high pressure for 6 minutes.
6. Quick release and stir well.
7. Plate both pasta dishes, garnishing with fresh herbs.

Nutritional Facts: (Per serving)

- ❖ Calories: 550
- ❖ Protein: 25g
- ❖ Carbohydrates: 60g
- ❖ Dietary Fiber: 3g
- ❖ Sugars: 5g
- ❖ Fat: 25g
- ❖ Cholesterol: 80mg
- ❖ Sodium: 500mg

Finish your evening with a taste of Italy, made effortlessly in the Instant Pot. This duo of pasta dishes promises warmth and satisfaction and a healthy dose of protein to fuel your day. Bon appétit!

Recipe 48: Grilled Pork Kebab With Red and Yellow Pepper

SERVINGS: 4

PREPPING TIME: 20 MINUTES

COOK TIME: 15 MINUTES

DIFFICULTY: INTERMEDIATE

This Grilled Pork Kebab with Red and Yellow Pepper offers a colorful and succulent blend of flavors that will delight your palate. Perfect for those looking for a high-protein meal, this dish comes together quickly in an Instant Pot for a fuss-free dinner.

Ingredients:

- ✓ 500g pork tenderloin, cubed
- ✓ 1 red bell pepper, cut into squares
- ✓ 1 yellow bell pepper, cut into squares
- ✓ 2 tablespoons olive oil
- ✓ 2 cloves garlic, minced
- ✓ 1 tablespoon lemon juice
- ✓ 1 teaspoon paprika
- ✓ Salt and pepper, to taste
- ✓ Fresh parsley for garnish

Step-by-Step Preparation:

1. Mix olive oil, garlic, lemon juice, paprika, salt, and pepper in a bowl. Add in pork cubes and marinate for 10 minutes.

2. After marination, thread the pork and bell peppers alternately onto skewers.

3. Set the Instant Pot to the sauté function and grill each skewer for 3-4 minutes on each side or until fully cooked and charred.

4. Once cooked, remove the kebabs and let them rest for a few minutes.

5. Garnish with fresh parsley before serving.

Nutritional Facts: (Per serving)

- ❖ Calories: 300
- ❖ Protein: 26g
- ❖ Carbs: 8g
- ❖ Fats: 18g
- ❖ Sugars: 4g
- ❖ Fiber: 2g

Indulge in a vibrant, savory delight with these Grilled Pork Kebabs. The combination of tender pork and crispy bell peppers offers a delightful texture and flavor. It is pleasing to the eyes and guarantees a satisfying, protein-rich meal in just a matter of minutes with the help of your trusty Instant Pot. Enjoy your meal!

Recipe 49: Creamy Tortellini the Soup With Chicken and Tomato

SERVINGS: 4

PREPPING TIME: 10 MINUTES

COOK TIME: 20 MINUTES

DIFFICULTY: EASY

Indulge in the comforting embrace of this creamy tortellini soup, brimming with tender chicken and robust tomatoes. This high-protein delight is prepared in an Instant Pot and is perfect for those seeking a wholesome yet quick dinner.

Ingredients:

- ✓ 1 pound boneless, skinless chicken breasts, diced
- ✓ 1 cup fresh tortellini pasta
- ✓ 2 cups chicken broth
- ✓ 1 can (14 oz) diced tomatoes
- ✓ 1 cup heavy cream
- ✓ 1 onion, finely chopped
- ✓ 3 cloves garlic, minced
- ✓ 2 tbsp olive oil
- ✓ 1 tsp dried basil
- ✓ 1 tsp dried oregano
- ✓ Salt and pepper to taste
- ✓ Fresh parsley for garnish

Step-by-Step Preparation:

1. Turn on the Instant Pot to the sauté setting. Add olive oil, onion, and garlic. Sauté until onions are translucent.

2. Add the diced chicken and brown slightly.

3. Stir in the diced tomatoes, chicken broth, basil, oregano, salt, and pepper.

4. Close the Instant Pot lid and set it to manual high pressure for 10 minutes.

5. Release pressure naturally for 5 minutes, then quick release.

6. Turn back to sauté mode and add in the tortellini. Cook until they float to the top.

7. Stir in the heavy cream until well combined and heated through.

8. Garnish with fresh parsley before serving.

Nutritional Facts: (Per serving)

- ❖ Calories: 420
- ❖ Protein: 30g
- ❖ Carbohydrates: 25g
- ❖ Dietary Fiber: 3g
- ❖ Sugars: 5g
- ❖ Fat: 20g
- ❖ Cholesterol: 110mg
- ❖ Sodium: 580mg

Savor the harmonious blend of flavors in this rich and filling soup. Perfect for chilly evenings or when you need comfort, the Creamy Tortellini Soup with Chicken and Tomato will indeed become a family favorite. The Instant Pot does all the heavy lifting, making it easy to enjoy a delicious meal any night of the week.

Recipe 50: Gratin With Spinach, Red Lentils and Wild Garlic

SERVINGS: 4

PREPPING TIME: 15 MINUTES

COOK TIME: 20 MINUTES

DIFFICULTY: EASY

Discover this rich, gratin, flavorful fusion of spinach, red lentils, and wild garlic. Perfect for those seeking high-protein dishes, this Instant Pot dinner is both nourishing and delectable.

Ingredients:

- ✓ 1 cup red lentils, rinsed and drained
- ✓ 2 cups fresh spinach, chopped
- ✓ 1 cup wild garlic, finely chopped
- ✓ 2 cups vegetable broth
- ✓ 1 cup grated parmesan cheese
- ✓ 1/2 cup heavy cream
- ✓ 2 tbsp olive oil
- ✓ Salt and pepper to taste

Step-by-Step Preparation:

1. Turn the Instant Pot on 'Sauté' mode. Add olive oil, spinach, and wild garlic. Sauté until wilted.

2. Add red lentils to the pot and stir.

3. Pour in the vegetable broth, ensuring the lentils are submerged.

4. Seal the Instant Pot lid and set it to 'Pressure Cook' for 15 minutes.

5. Release pressure, open the lid, and stir in heavy cream and parmesan cheese.

6. Season with salt and pepper. Transfer to a baking dish, sprinkle more cheese if desired, and broil for 3-5 minutes until golden on top.

Nutritional Facts: (Per serving)

- ❖ Calories: 350
- ❖ Protein: 20g
- ❖ Carbs: 40g
- ❖ Fat: 15g
- ❖ Fiber: 10g
- ❖ Sugar: 3g

Indulge in this heartwarming gratin that celebrates earthy flavors and rich textures. It's delightful to the palate and packed with proteins, making it a healthful dinner choice. Whether an Instant Pot pro or a newbie, this dish will be favored in your culinary repertoire.

Recipe 51: Homemade Mug Cakes With Protein Topping

SERVINGS: 2

PREPPING TIME: 5 MINUTES

COOK TIME: 10 MINUTES

DIFFICULTY: EASY

Indulge in a delectable and nutritious treat with these Homemade Mug Cakes topped with a protein-rich finish. Perfect for those midnight snack cravings, this Instant Pot recipe is quick to whip up and will satisfy your sweet tooth without derailing your fitness goals.

Ingredients:

- ✓ 4 tablespoons all-purpose flour
- ✓ 2 tablespoons unsweetened cocoa powder
- ✓ 4 tablespoons sugar or sweetener of choice
- ✓ 1/8 teaspoon baking powder
- ✓ A pinch of salt
- ✓ 3 tablespoons milk of choice
- ✓ 2 tablespoons vegetable oil
- ✓ 1/4 teaspoon vanilla extract
- ✓ 2 tablespoons protein powder (for topping)
- ✓ 4 tablespoons Greek yogurt (for topping)

Step-by-Step Preparation:

1. Mix flour, cocoa powder, sugar, baking powder, and salt in a bowl.
2. Stir in milk, vegetable oil, and vanilla extract until smooth.
3. Pour the mixture into two mugs, filling only half.
4. Place the mugs inside the Instant Pot, ensuring they don't touch each other.
5. Set the Instant Pot to "Manual" and cook for 10 minutes.
6. While the cakes are cooking, mix protein powder with Greek yogurt to make the topping.
7. Once done, carefully remove mugs from the Instant Pot and let cool for a minute.
8. Top with the protein mixture and serve immediately.

Nutritional Facts: (Per serving)

- ❖ Calories: 280
- ❖ Protein: 12g
- ❖ Carbohydrates: 35g
- ❖ Dietary Fiber: 2g
- ❖ Sugars: 20g
- ❖ Fat: 12g
- ❖ Cholesterol: 5mg
- ❖ Sodium: 90mg

Rejoice in the delightful fusion of moist cake and protein-packed topping with this mug cake recipe. Ideal for late-night snacking, it's not just delicious but also a healthier alternative. So, the next time you crave a sweet treat, remember this quick and easy recipe and enjoy a guilt-free indulgence.

Recipe 52: Pulled Chicken and Cheddar Quesadillas

SERVINGS:4

PREPPING TIME: 15 MINUTES

COOK TIME: 30 MINUTES

DIFFICULTY: EASY

Craving a high-protein treat late at night? These pulled chicken and cheddar quesadillas prepared in an Instant Pot are your perfect solution. Quick to make, they combine the rich flavors of tender chicken and melted cheddar in a crispy tortilla.

Ingredients:

- ✓ 2 large boneless chicken breasts
- ✓ 1 cup shredded cheddar cheese
- ✓ 4 large tortillas
- ✓ 1/2 cup salsa (optional for added flavor)
- ✓ 1 tsp ground cumin
- ✓ 1 tsp chili powder
- ✓ 1/2 tsp garlic powder
- ✓ Salt and pepper to taste
- ✓ 2 tbsp olive oil

Step-by-Step Preparation:

1. Place chicken breasts in the Instant Pot with salt, pepper, cumin, chili powder, and garlic powder.
2. Cook on high pressure for 20 minutes, then release steam.
3. Once cooled, shred the chicken with forks.
4. Preheat a skillet and brush with olive oil.
5. Lay out the tortilla, spread a layer of shredded chicken, sprinkle with cheddar, and fold in half.
6. Cook until crispy and golden on both sides.
7. Serve with salsa if desired.

Nutritional Facts: (Per serving)

- ❖ Calories: 320
- ❖ Protein: 28g
- ❖ Carbohydrates: 22g
- ❖ Fats: 12g
- ❖ Sodium: 520mg
- ❖ Fiber: 1g

There's no longer any need to deny those midnight munchies. These protein-packed quesadillas are satisfying and flavorful and give your body the nutrient boost it craves. They'll soon become your go-to late-night snack and are quick, delicious, and easy to make.

Recipe 53: Crispy Tortilla Chips

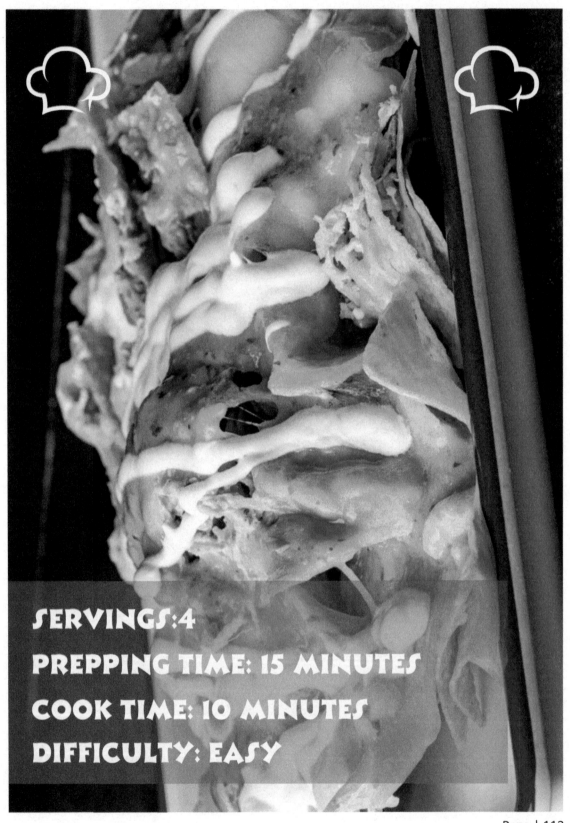

SERVINGS: 4

PREPPING TIME: 15 MINUTES

COOK TIME: 10 MINUTES

DIFFICULTY: EASY

Late-night cravings deserve a fulfilling touch, and nothing hits the spot quite like these high-protein Instant Pot tortilla nachos. This recipe combines the richness of meat with the freshness of salsa and guacamole, delivering a harmonious blend of flavors that's sure to satisfy.

Ingredients:

✓ Tortilla chips: 200g

✓ Cheddar cheese (shredded): 2 cups

✓ Salsa: 1 cup

✓ Cooked meat (chicken/beef): 1 cup

✓ Black beans: ½ cup

✓ Jalapenos (sliced): ¼ cup

✓ Guacamole: ½ cup

✓ Sour cream: ½ cup

✓ Lettuce (shredded): 1 cup

Step-by-Step Preparation:

1. Arrange tortilla chips on a serving plate or tray.

2. Sprinkle shredded cheddar cheese evenly over the chips.

3. Layer the meat and black beans over the cheese.

4. Set the Instant Pot to "Sauté" mode and melt the cheese until it's bubbly and golden.

5. Top with generous dollops of salsa, guacamole, and sour cream.

6. Garnish with jalapenos and shredded lettuce.

7. Serve immediately and enjoy!

Nutritional Facts: (Per serving)

❖ Calories: 465

❖ Protein: 23g

❖ Carbs: 45g

❖ Fat: 23g

❖ Fiber: 8g

❖ Sugars: 4g

When midnight hunger strikes, there's no need to compromise on taste or nutrition. This Instant Pot nacho dish satisfies those late-night munchies and packs a protein punch to keep you full and fueled. Next time the clock strikes twelve, remember this recipe and treat yourself to a sumptuous delight.

Recipe 54: Toffee Macadamia Nut Cake

SERVINGS:4

PREPPING TIME: 15 MINUTES

COOK TIME: 25 MINUTES

DIFFICULTY: MODERATE

This decadent Toffee Macadamia Nut Cake isn't just a treat for the taste buds. Loaded with protein and the convenience of the Instant Pot, it's perfect for those midnight cravings that need a healthy twist. Let's indulge while staying on track!

Ingredients:

- ✓ 1 cup almond flour
- ✓ 1/4 cup protein powder (vanilla or unflavored)
- ✓ 1/2 cup macadamia nuts, roughly chopped
- ✓ 1/4 cup unsalted butter, melted
- ✓ 1/2 cup toffee bits

- ✓ 2 large eggs
- ✓ 1/4 cup almond milk
- ✓ 1 tsp vanilla extract
- ✓ 1/4 tsp baking soda
- ✓ Pinch of salt

Step-by-Step Preparation:

1. Combine almond flour, protein powder, baking soda, and salt in a mixing bowl.

2. Whisk together eggs, almond milk, melted butter, and vanilla extract in another bowl.

3. Mix wet ingredients into dry, then fold in toffee bits and macadamia nuts.

4. Pour the batter into a greased Instant Pot-safe cake pan.

5. Set Instant Pot to pressure cook for 25 minutes manually.

6. Once done, release pressure naturally. Remove the cake and let it cool slightly before serving.

Nutritional Facts: (Per serving)

- ❖ Calories: 320
- ❖ Protein: 15g
- ❖ Carbs: 25g
- ❖ Fat: 20g
- ❖ Sugar: 15g
- ❖ Fiber: 3g

Enjoy this warm, delightful cake's harmonious blend of crunchy macadamia and sticky toffee. Not only does this recipe satisfy those late-night dessert urges, but it also packs a protein punch. Slice, savor, and let this Instant Pot magic become your go-to midnight snack!

Recipe 55: Baked Chicken Breast Stuffed With Cheese and Spinach

SERVINGS: 4

PREPPING TIME: 15 MINUTES

COOK TIME: 20 MINUTES

DIFFICULTY: EASY

Satisfy your late-night cravings with this high-protein delight! Our Baked Chicken Breast Stuffed with Cheese and Spinach is a savory concoction that effortlessly marries nutrition with indulgence. Let the Instant Pot make your midnight snack prep a breeze.

Ingredients:

- ✓ 4 boneless, skinless chicken breasts
- ✓ 1 cup fresh spinach, chopped
- ✓ 1/2 cup ricotta cheese
- ✓ 1/4 cup Parmesan cheese, grated
- ✓ 2 cloves garlic, minced
- ✓ 1 tsp olive oil
- ✓ Salt and pepper to taste
- ✓ 1/2 tsp paprika

Step-by-Step Preparation:

1. Combine spinach, ricotta, Parmesan, and garlic in a mixing bowl. Mix until smooth.

2. Cut a slit in the side of each chicken breast to create a pocket. Stuff each pocket with the spinach and cheese mixture.

3. Season chicken breasts with salt, pepper, and paprika.

4. Pour olive oil into the Instant Pot. Place chicken breasts inside.

5. Set the Instant Pot to the poultry setting and cook for 15 minutes.

6. Once done, allow a natural release for 5 minutes before quickly releasing the remaining pressure.

Nutritional Facts: (Per serving)

- ❖ Calories: 270
- ❖ Protein: 30g
- ❖ Carbohydrates: 3g
- ❖ Fat: 14g
- ❖ Fiber: 1g
- ❖ Sugars: 1g
- ❖ Sodium: 300mg

This Baked Chicken Breast Stuffed with Cheese and Spinach is the ideal blend of creamy, savory, and protein-packed goodness. Quick and convenient, it's the perfect high-protein Instant Pot dish to elevate your midnight snacking experience. Enjoy its warmth and richness anytime you desire!

Recipe 56: Vegan Chocolate Chip Pankcakes

SERVINGS:2

PREPPING TIME: 10 MINUTES

COOK TIME: 15 MINUTES

DIFFICULTY: EASY

Indulge your midnight cravings with this high-protein, vegan delight. These chocolate chip pancakes made effortlessly in your Instant Pot, are satisfying and healthy. The syrup drizzle adds a touch of sweetness to that perfect late-night treat.

Ingredients:

- ✓ 1 cup chickpea flour
- ✓ 1/2 cup almond milk
- ✓ 1/4 cup vegan chocolate chips
- ✓ 1 tsp baking powder
- ✓ 1/4 tsp salt
- ✓ 2 tbsp maple syrup
- ✓ 1 tbsp coconut oil
- ✓ 1 tsp vanilla extract

Step-by-Step Preparation:

1. Mix chickpea flour, baking powder, and salt in a bowl.
2. Add almond milk, coconut oil, and vanilla extract. Stir until smooth.
3. Fold in the vegan chocolate chips.
4. Pour the batter into the Instant Pot, ensuring an even layer.
5. Cook on the "Sauté" setting until bubbles form, then flip and cook the other side.
6. Serve hot, drizzled with maple syrup.

Nutritional Facts: (Per serving)

- ❖ Calories: 280
- ❖ Protein: 12g
- ❖ Carbs: 35g
- ❖ Fat: 12g
- ❖ Fiber: 4g
- ❖ Sugars: 15g

As midnight draws near, satiate those hunger pangs with this delectable snack. The decadent chocolate chips and sweet syrup blend offers a delightful contrast to the savory chickpea pancakes. Dive in and experience a delicious, protein-rich treat for any late-night adventure.

Recipe 57: Meat Chicken and Ham and Cheese Empanadas

SERVINGS: 6

PREPPING TIME: 20 MINUTES

COOK TIME: 15 MINUTES

DIFFICULTY: MEDIUM

Craving a late-night bite with a protein punch? Dive into this delicious Meat, Chicken, Ham, and Cheese Empanadas. Made effortlessly in the Instant Pot, these treats are the perfect amalgamation of flavors and textures to satisfy your midnight hunger pangs.

Ingredients:

- ✓ 2 cups shredded cooked chicken
- ✓ 1 cup diced ham
- ✓ 1 cup shredded cheese (cheddar or mozzarella)
- ✓ 1 pack of ready-made empanada dough
- ✓ 1/2 cup chopped onions
- ✓ 2 cloves garlic, minced
- ✓ 2 tbsp olive oil
- ✓ Salt and pepper to taste

Step-by-Step Preparation:

1. Turn on the Instant Pot and select the Sauté function. Add olive oil.
2. Sauté onions and garlic until translucent.
3. Add chicken, ham, seasonings, and sauté for 3-4 minutes.
4. Turn off the Instant Pot. Let the mixture cool.
5. Roll out empanada dough, fill with chicken-ham mixture, and sprinkle cheese.
6. Fold and seal the empanadas.
7. Place empanadas in the Instant Pot and cook on manual high pressure for 8 minutes.
8. Release pressure and serve hot.

Nutritional Facts: (Per serving)

- ❖ Calories: 280
- ❖ Protein: 21g
- ❖ Carbohydrates: 22g
- ❖ Fat: 12g
- ❖ Sodium: 480mg
- ❖ Fiber: 1g

These Chicken and Ham and Cheese Empanadas are more than just a snack; they're an experience. Combining the savory essence of chicken and ham with melted cheese bite is a journey of flavors. Perfect for those looking for a high-protein nibble in the middle of the night. Enjoy, and let every bite take you to culinary heaven!

Recipe 58: Crunchy Granola With Yogurt, Banana, Nuts, Chocolate and Honey

SERVINGS: 2

PREPPING TIME: 10 MINUTES

COOK TIME: 20 MINUTES

DIFFICULTY: EASY

When midnight hunger pangs hit, this Crunchy Granola with Yogurt and delectable toppings delivers a satisfying, protein-rich treat. The Instant Pot makes whipping this snack quick and delightful, making your nocturnal nibbles healthier and tastier.

Ingredients:

- ✓ 1 cup granola
- ✓ 2 cups Greek yogurt
- ✓ 1 ripe banana, sliced
- ✓ ¼ cup mixed nuts (almonds, walnuts, etc.)
- ✓ ¼ cup chocolate chunks or chips
- ✓ 2 tbsp honey

Step-by-Step Preparation:

1. Start by placing granola into the Instant Pot and give it a quick toast for 2 minutes on sauté mode.
2. Remove the granola from the Instant Pot and let it cool.
3. In serving bowls, layer Greek yogurt as the base.
4. Top with toasted granola, followed by banana slices.
5. Sprinkle nuts and chocolate chunks or chips over the top.
6. Finally, drizzle honey over everything for a touch of sweetness.

Nutritional Facts: (Per serving)

- ❖ Calories: 450
- ❖ Protein: 20g
- ❖ Carbohydrates: 50g
- ❖ Fat: 20g
- ❖ Sugars: 25g
- ❖ Fiber: 5g

This Crunchy Granola delight perfectly merges the indulgence of midnight snacks with health-conscious choices. It's a dish that satisfies cravings and provides energy and protein. Whether a treat after a late-night workout or simply an indulgence, this snack proves you don't have to compromise flavor for nutrition. Enjoy!

Recipe 59: Chocolate Peanut Butter, Cocoa and Vegan Brownie Toast With Sliced Banana and Cinnamon

SERVINGS: 4

PREPPING TIME: 15 MINUTES

COOK TIME: 25 MINUTES

DIFFICULTY: MEDIUM

Indulge in a heavenly fusion of flavors with this Chocolate Peanut Butter, Cocoa, and Vegan Brownie. Paired with a crispy toast topped with fresh banana slices and a sprinkle of cinnamon high-protein treat, it is perfect for those late-night cravings.

Ingredients:

- ✓ 1/2 cup dark cocoa powder
- ✓ 1 cup peanut butter
- ✓ 1 cup almond flour
- ✓ 3/4 cup maple syrup
- ✓ 2 tsp vanilla extract

- ✓ 1/2 tsp baking soda
- ✓ Pinch of salt
- ✓ 4 slices of whole-grain bread
- ✓ 2 bananas, sliced
- ✓ 1 tsp ground cinnamon

Step-by-Step Preparation:

1. Mix cocoa powder, peanut butter, almond flour, maple syrup, vanilla, baking soda, and salt in a bowl.
2. Pour mixture into a greased Instant Pot liner.
3. Set Instant Pot on "High Pressure" for 25 minutes.
4. Once cooked, release pressure and let it cool.
5. Toast the bread slices.
6. Top toast with banana slices and sprinkle with cinnamon.
7. Serve with a slice of the brownie.

Nutritional Facts: (Per serving)

- ❖ Calories: 350
- ❖ Protein: 12g
- ❖ Carbs: 45g
- ❖ Fat: 18g
- ❖ Fiber: 6g
- ❖ Sugars: 25g

Dive into this delightful snack, blending the richness of chocolate with the creamy goodness of peanut butter, elevated by the wholesome taste of bananas on toast. This dish promises a burst of flavor and a nutritional boost to keep you going, even past midnight. Enjoy!

Recipe 60: Chocolate Protein Orange Slices Overnight Oats

SERVINGS: 2

PREPPING TIME: 10 MINUTES

COOK TIME: 20 MINUTES

DIFFICULTY: EASY

Indulge in the delightful blend of chocolate and oranges with our Chocolate Protein Orange Slices Overnight Oats. Perfect for late-night hunger pangs, this dish satisfies your sweet cravings and packs a protein punch.

Ingredients:

- ✓ 1 cup rolled oats
- ✓ 2 cups almond milk
- ✓ 1/4 cup chocolate protein powder
- ✓ Zest and juice of 1 orange
- ✓ 2 tbsp honey or maple syrup
- ✓ 1/2 tsp vanilla extract
- ✓ Pinch of salt
- ✓ Orange slices for garnish
- ✓ Chocolate shavings (optional)

Step-by-Step Preparation:

1. Combine oats, chocolate protein powder, orange zest, and salt in a bowl.
2. Stir in almond milk, honey or maple syrup, and vanilla extract.
3. Pour the mixture into the Instant Pot.
4. Set the Instant Pot on 'Low' and cook for 20 minutes.
5. Once cooked, let it cool slightly. Stir in the orange juice.
6. Transfer to bowls or jars and refrigerate overnight.
7. Garnish with orange slices and optional chocolate shavings before serving.

Nutritional Facts: (Per serving)

- ❖ Calories: 320
- ❖ Protein: 15g
- ❖ Carbohydrates: 50g
- ❖ Dietary Fiber: 7g
- ❖ Sugars: 20g
- ❖ Fat: 5g
- ❖ Sodium: 100mg

Bid farewell to midnight hunger with our Chocolate Protein Orange Slices Overnight Oats. Not just a treat for your taste buds, this snack keeps you fueled with essential nutrients. Whether you're pulling an all-nighter or need a tasty pick-me-up, this Instant Pot delight won't disappoint.

Chapter 07: Protein-Infused Indulgences

Recipe 61: Chocolate Cake With Protein Decorated With Berries

SERVINGS: 8

PREPPING TIME: 20 MINUTES

COOK TIME: 30 MINUTES

DIFFICULTY: MODERATE

With a protein twist, this decadent Chocolate Cake is a delectable treat for fitness enthusiasts. It's not just a dessert but infused with luscious flavors and topped with fresh berries. It's a statement of health-meets-indulgence made in an Instant Pot.

Ingredients:

- ✓ 2 cups almond flour
- ✓ 1 cup cocoa powder
- ✓ 3/4 cup honey or maple syrup
- ✓ 4 eggs
- ✓ 1/2 cup unsweetened almond milk
- ✓ 2 tsp baking powder
- ✓ 1 scoop protein powder (chocolate or vanilla flavor)
- ✓ 1 tsp vanilla extract
- ✓ Pinch of salt
- ✓ Mixed berries for decoration (blueberries, raspberries, strawberries)

Step-by-Step Preparation:

1. Mix almond flour, cocoa powder, baking powder, protein powder, and salt in a large bowl.
2. Whisk eggs, honey/maple syrup, almond milk, and vanilla extract in another bowl.
3. Merge the wet and dry ingredients, ensuring a smooth batter.
4. Pour the mixture into a greased Instant Pot pan.
5. Set Instant Pot to 'Manual' mode and cook for 30 minutes.
6. Once done, release the pressure and let the cake cool.
7. Decorate with fresh berries on top.

Nutritional Facts: (Per serving)

- ❖ Calories: 285
- ❖ Protein: 12g
- ❖ Carbs: 32g
- ❖ Fat: 14g
- ❖ Fiber: 5g
- ❖ Sugars: 20g

Who said indulging in chocolate cake can't be healthy? This high-protein dessert delivers not just on flavor but also on nutrition. The harmonious blend of cocoa and berries ensures you get antioxidants, while the protein content keeps your muscles happy. Enjoy without guilt!

Recipe 62: Panna Cotta Berry Fitness Dessert

SERVINGS: 4

PREPPING TIME: 15 MINUTES

COOK TIME: 20 MINUTES

DIFFICULTY: EASY

Indulge your sweet cravings with this "Panna Cotta Berry Fitness Dessert." Comprising three delightful layers – coffee, vanilla, and berry – this milk jelly pudding is not just a treat for the eyes but also loaded with protein. Made effortlessly in an Instant Pot, it's the perfect end to any meal.

Ingredients:

- ✓ 2 cups of low-fat milk
- ✓ 2 tbsp gelatin powder
- ✓ 1/4 cup cold water
- ✓ 1/2 cup of honey or preferred sweetener
- • 1/2 cup of protein powder
- ✓ 1 tsp vanilla extract
- ✓ 1 tsp instant coffee granules
- ✓ 1/2 cup of mixed berries (blueberries, raspberries, strawberries)

Step-by-Step Preparation:

1. In a bowl, sprinkle gelatin over cold water; let stand for 5 minutes.
2. In the Instant Pot, combine milk, honey, and protein powder. Stir until smooth.
3. Add the gelatin mixture to the Instant Pot and whisk.
4. Divide the mixture into three equal parts.
5. In the first part, mix in the vanilla extract.
6. In the second, stir in the instant coffee granules.
7. In the third, blend in the berries.
8. Pour each mixture separately into dessert glasses, allowing each layer to set before adding the next.
9. Chill for at least 2 hours or until set.

Nutritional Facts: (Per serving)

- ❖ Calories: 220
- ❖ Protein: 12g
- ❖ Carbohydrates: 32g
- ❖ Sugars: 25g
- ❖ Fat: 4g
- ❖ Fiber: 1g
- ❖ Sodium: 50mg

Revel in the delight of this three-layered Panna Cotta Berry Fitness Dessert. This Instant Pot creation shows that desserts can be delicious and nutritious, perfect for those looking to balance health and indulgence. Serve chilled, and enjoy the symphony of flavors!

Recipe 63: Mixed Fruit Loaf Cake

SERVINGS: 8

PREPPING TIME: 15 MINUTES

COOK TIME: 40 MINUTES

DIFFICULTY: MEDIUM

Dive into the delightful Instant Pot desserts with this Mixed Fruit Loaf Cake. Packed with an assortment of fruits and a boost of protein loaf is not just delectable but also nourishing. Perfect for those who wish to satisfy their sweet tooth without any guilt!

Ingredients:

- ✓ 1 ½ cups mixed dried fruits (raisins, apricots, cranberries)
- ✓ 2 cups whole wheat flour
- ✓ 1 scoop protein powder (vanilla or unflavored)
- ✓ ½ cup honey or agave nectar
- ✓ 2 large eggs
- ✓ 1 tsp baking powder
- ✓ ½ tsp baking soda
- ✓ 1 cup Greek yogurt
- ✓ 1 tsp vanilla extract
- ✓ ¼ tsp salt
- ✓ 1 tbsp coconut oil (for greasing)

Step-by-Step Preparation:

1. In a large mixing bowl, combine the whole wheat flour, protein powder, baking powder, baking soda, and salt.

2. Whisk together the eggs, honey, Greek yogurt, and vanilla extract in a separate bowl.

3. Gradually add the wet ingredients to the dry ingredients, mixing until combined.

4. Fold in the mixed dried fruits.

5. Grease the Instant Pot insert with coconut oil.

6. Pour the batter into the pot.

7. Seal the Instant Pot lid and set it to manual high pressure for 40 minutes.

8. Once cooked, release pressure naturally and let the cake cool before slicing.

Nutritional Facts: (Per serving)

- ❖ Calories: 265
- ❖ Protein: 10g
- ❖ Carbohydrates: 50g
- ❖ Fat: 5g
- ❖ Fiber: 4g
- ❖ Sugars: 25g
- ❖ Sodium: 120mg

This Mixed Fruit Loaf Cake is a game-changer for health-conscious dessert enthusiasts. The Instant Pot ensures a moist, perfectly baked texture, while the combination of fruits and protein makes it a wholesome treat. Slice it up for breakfast, dessert, or a mid-day snack; it's versatile, delightful, and undeniably nutritious!

Recipe 64: Apple Cinnamon Protein Crumble

SERVINGS: 4

PREPPING TIME: 15 MINUTES

COOK TIME: 20 MINUTES

DIFFICULTY: EASY

Indulge your sweet tooth without any guilt with this Apple Cinnamon Protein Crumble. Using an Instant Pot, this dessert is high in protein and quick and easy to prepare, ensuring a delightful treat for any fitness enthusiast.

Ingredients:

- ✓ 4 medium apples, peeled and sliced
- ✓ 2 scoops vanilla protein powder
- ✓ 1 cup old-fashioned oats
- ✓ 1/2 cup almond flour
- ✓ 1/4 cup honey or maple syrup
- ✓ 2 tsp cinnamon
- ✓ 1/4 tsp nutmeg
- ✓ 1/4 cup melted coconut oil
- ✓ Pinch of salt

Step-by-Step Preparation:

1. In a mixing bowl, combine apples with honey (or maple syrup), cinnamon, and nutmeg.

2. Pour the apple mixture into the Instant Pot.

3. Combine oats, protein powder, almond flour, coconut oil, and salt in another bowl. Mix until a crumbly texture is achieved.

4. Sprinkle the crumble over the apple mixture in the Instant Pot.

5. Secure the lid and set the pot to manual mode, high pressure, for 20 minutes.

6. Release pressure naturally before serving.

Nutritional Facts: (Per serving)

- ❖ Calories: 320
- ❖ Protein: 15g
- ❖ Carbohydrates: 45g
- ❖ Fat: 12g
- ❖ Fiber: 5g
- ❖ Sugars: 25g

This Apple Cinnamon Protein Crumble is more than a delightful dessert. Its high protein content and wholesome ingredients make it a splendid fusion of taste and nutrition. Dive into a bowl post-workout or whenever you crave a touch of sweetness, and enjoy the perfect balance between indulgence and health.

Recipe 65: Gluten Free Vegan Avocado Blueberry Muffins

SERVINGS: 12

PREPPING TIME: 15 MINUTES

COOK TIME: 20 MINUTES

DIFFICULTY: EASY

Indulge in the decadent fusion of ripe blueberries and creamy avocado with these Gluten-Free Vegan Avocado Blueberry Muffins. Using chickpea flour as a protein-packed base delightful treat is delicious and nutritious. Make it effortlessly in your Instant Pot and savor the flavors of health and sweetness combined.

Ingredients:

- ✓ 2 ripe avocados, mashed
- ✓ 1 cup fresh blueberries
- ✓ 2 cups chickpea flour (besan)
- ✓ 1/2 cup coconut sugar (or any sweetener of choice)
- ✓ 1 tsp baking soda
- ✓ 1/2 tsp salt
- ✓ 1/4 cup coconut oil, melted
- ✓ 1 tsp vanilla extract
- ✓ 1/4 cup almond milk

Step-by-Step Preparation:

1. Combine mashed avocados, coconut oil, and coconut sugar in a mixing bowl until smooth.
2. Add chickpea flour, baking soda, salt, and vanilla extract. Mix well.
3. Slowly pour in almond milk, blending until a smooth batter forms.
4. Gently fold in the blueberries.
5. Pour the batter into silicone muffin cups or a greased muffin tin.
6. Place the tin in the Instant Pot and cook on "Steam" for 20 minutes.
7. Once done, allow the muffins to cool for 10 minutes before removing.

Nutritional Facts: (Per serving)

- ❖ Calories: 150
- ❖ Protein: 5g
- ❖ Carbs: 20g
- ❖ Fiber: 3g
- ❖ Sugars: 8g
- ❖ Fat: 7g
- ❖ Saturated Fat: 3g
- ❖ Sodium: 120mg

Embrace the perfect blend of taste and nutrition with these Gluten-Free Vegan Avocado Blueberry Muffins. Whether for breakfast or a mid-day treat, these muffins provide a protein-rich experience without compromising flavor. Let your Instant Pot do the magic, and enjoy the harmony of creamy avocado, juicy blueberries, and the richness of chickpea flour in every bite.

Recipe 66: Baked Pavlova Meringue Cake With Lemon Layer

SERVINGS: 8

PREPPING TIME: 15 MINUTES

COOK TIME: 45 MINUTES

DIFFICULTY: MEDIUM

Indulge in the delightful balance of crispy and zesty lemon with the baked pavlova meringue cake. This high-protein dessert, cooked effortlessly in the Instant Pot, will leave your tastebuds tingling and craving more. A dream for dessert lovers!

Ingredients:

- ✓ 6 large egg whites
- ✓ 1 1/2 cups granulated sugar
- ✓ 1 tsp white vinegar
- ✓ 1 tsp cornstarch
- ✓ 1 tsp vanilla extract
- ✓ Zest of 2 lemons
- ✓ 1 cup Greek yogurt
- ✓ 2 tbsp honey
- ✓ Fresh berries for garnish

Step-by-Step Preparation:

1. In a clean bowl, whisk egg whites until stiff peaks form.
2. Gradually add sugar, whisking continuously.
3. Fold in vinegar, cornstarch, vanilla extract, and lemon zest.
4. Transfer the mixture into the Instant Pot, smoothening the top.
5. Set Instant Pot on high for 45 minutes.
6. Once done, allow it to cool and release naturally.
7. Mix Greek yogurt and honey and spread over the meringue.
8. Garnish with fresh berries.

Nutritional Facts: (Per serving)

- ❖ Calories: 210
- ❖ Protein: 6g
- ❖ Carbs: 40g
- ❖ Sugars: 38g
- ❖ Fat: 1g
- ❖ Fiber: 0.5g

Elevate your dessert experience with this baked pavlova meringue cake. The tangy lemon layer perfectly complements the sweet, crisp meringue. It's not just a dessert. It's a symphony of flavors! Delight your guests and make any occasion memorable with this exquisite Instant Pot masterpiece.

Recipe 67: Healthy Energy Protein Balls

SERVINGS: 4

PREPPING TIME: 15 MINUTES

COOK TIME: 10 MINUTES

DIFFICULTY: EASY

Indulge in a delicious treat that satisfies your sweet cravings and boosts your energy! These healthy protein balls combine the goodness of dates, oats, peanut butter, and dark chocolate, presented as gluten-free truffle bites. Either dusted with cocoa powder or rolled in almonds, these are perfect for a post-workout snack or a healthy dessert.

Ingredients:

- ✓ 1 cup pitted dates
- ✓ 1/2 cup rolled oats (gluten-free)
- ✓ 1/4 cup peanut butter
- ✓ 1/4 cup dark chocolate chips
- ✓ 2 tbsp chia seeds (optional)
- ✓ 2 tbsp flaxseeds (optional)
- ✓ 2 tbsp unsweetened cocoa powder (for dusting)
- ✓ 1/4 cup crushed almonds (for rolling)

Step-by-Step Preparation:

1. Blend dates in a processor until they form a sticky mixture.
2. Mix oats, peanut butter, dark chocolate chips, chia seeds, and flaxseeds in a bowl.
3. Combine the date mixture with the oat mixture and mix until well combined.
4. Form the mixture into small balls.
5. Place balls in the Instant Pot on low pressure for 10 minutes.
6. Once cooled, roll in cocoa powder or crushed almonds.

Nutritional Facts: (Per serving)

- ❖ Calories: 110
- ❖ Protein: 4g
- ❖ Carbohydrates: 16g
- ❖ Dietary Fiber: 3g
- ❖ Sugars: 10g
- ❖ Fat: 5g
- ❖ Sodium: 10mg

Relish the delectable fusion of flavors and textures with these protein-packed energy balls! Perfect for fitness enthusiasts or those on the go, these truffle bites look gourmet and offer nutritional benefits. With the simplicity of the Instant Pot, creating these healthful treats has never been easier or more delightful.

Recipe 68: Strawberry Lemonade Bars

SERVINGS: 6

PREPPING TIME: 15 MINUTES

COOK TIME: 25 MINUTES

DIFFICULTY: MODERATE

A delightful twist on traditional dessert bars, these Strawberry Lemonade Bars combine the sweetness of strawberries with the tang of lemonade. Using the Instant Pot, they're delicious and high in protein. A perfect summer treat to refresh and nourish!

Ingredients:

- ✓ 1 cup of crushed graham crackers
- ✓ 4 tbsp melted butter
- ✓ 1/2 cup fresh strawberry puree
- ✓ 1/4 cup lemon juice
- ✓ 2 scoops of vanilla protein powder
- ✓ 1/2 cup Greek yogurt
- ✓ 3 eggs
- ✓ 1/4 cup honey or sweetener of choice

Step-by-Step Preparation:

1. Mix crushed graham crackers with melted butter and press into the base of the Instant Pot insert.

2. Whisk together strawberry puree, lemon juice, protein powder, Greek yogurt, eggs, and honey in a mixing bowl.

3. Pour the mixture over the crust.

4. Set Instant Pot to 'Manual' and cook for 25 minutes.

5. Allow natural release and then refrigerate for at least 3 hours.

6. Cut into bars and serve chilled.

Nutritional Facts: (Per serving)

- ❖ Calories: 230
- ❖ Protein: 14g
- ❖ Carbohydrates: 25g
- ❖ Fats: 8g
- ❖ Sugars: 15g
- ❖ Fiber: 1g

Indulge in a fruity zest and creaminess fusion without compromising your protein intake. Strawberry Lemonade Bars will not only satiate your sweet cravings but will also fuel your day. Perfect for a post-workout snack or a leisurely brunch, their vibrant taste and nutrition make them a must-try!

Recipe 69: Pumpkin Casserole With Apple and Semolina

SERVINGS: 4

PREPPING TIME: 15 MINUTES

COOK TIME: 20 MINUTES

DIFFICULTY: EASY

Indulge in a delightful fusion of pumpkin, apple, and semolina, packed with protein. This Instant Pot dessert brings the warmth of autumn flavors to your table, making it a perfect treat for cozy evenings.

Ingredients:

- ✓ 2 cups diced pumpkin
- ✓ 1 large apple, peeled and diced
- ✓ 1/2 cup semolina
- ✓ 2 cups milk
- ✓ 1/4 cup honey or maple syrup
- ✓ 1 tsp vanilla extract
- ✓ 1/2 tsp cinnamon powder
- ✓ 1/4 cup chopped walnuts
- ✓ 1/4 cup protein powder (optional for added protein)

Step-by-Step Preparation:

1. Combine diced pumpkin, apple, and milk in the Instant Pot.
2. Set to Manual mode and cook for 10 minutes.
3. Release pressure and open the lid. Stir in semolina.
4. Add honey, vanilla extract, and cinnamon. Mix well.
5. If using, fold in protein powder until well combined.
6. Sprinkle walnuts on top.
7. Set Instant Pot to Sauté mode and cook for another 10 minutes, stirring occasionally.
8. Serve warm.

Nutritional Facts: (Per serving)

- ❖ Calories: 280
- ❖ Protein: 12g (more if protein powder is added)
- ❖ Carbohydrates: 45g
- ❖ Fat: 7g
- ❖ Fiber: 4g
- ❖ Sugars: 20g

Immerse yourself in the delicious medley of pumpkin, apple, and semolina. This dessert satisfies your sweet cravings and nourishes your body with high-quality protein. Ideal for those looking to add a dash of health to their dessert choices!

Recipe 70: Raspberry and Banana With Chocolate Mousse

SERVINGS: 4

PREPPING TIME: 10 MINUTES

COOK TIME: 20 MINUTES

DIFFICULTY: EASY

Dive into a delightful combination of tangy raspberry and sweet banana enveloped in rich chocolate mousse. This high-protein dessert made in an Instant Pot will satisfy your sweet tooth while providing an unexpected protein punch. Perfect for health enthusiasts with a penchant for indulgence.

Ingredients:

- ✓ 200g dark chocolate, chopped
- ✓ 2 ripe bananas, mashed
- ✓ 1 cup fresh raspberries
- ✓ 3 egg whites
- ✓ 2 tbsp honey or agave nectar
- ✓ 1 tsp vanilla extract
- ✓ 2 tbsp protein powder (optional)
- ✓ Pinch of salt

Step-by-Step Preparation:

1. Place chopped chocolate in the Instant Pot and melt using the sauté function, stirring frequently.

2. Once melted, stir in the mashed bananas, honey/agave, and vanilla extract.

3. Whisk the egg whites with a pinch of salt in a separate bowl until stiff peaks form.

4. Gently fold the egg whites and protein powder (if using) into the chocolate mixture.

5. Layer the bottom of your serving dishes with raspberries.

6. Pour the chocolate mousse over the raspberries.

7. Seal the Instant Pot and set it on high pressure for 5 minutes. Allow natural release.

8. Once cooked, chill in the fridge for 2 hours before serving.

Nutritional Facts: (Per serving)

- ❖ Calories: 300
- ❖ Protein: 10g
- ❖ Carbs: 40g
- ❖ Dietary Fiber: 5g
- ❖ Sugars: 28g
- ❖ Fat: 12g

Elevate your dessert experience with this Raspberry and Banana Chocolate Mousse. Made effortlessly in an Instant Pot, this treat is sumptuously satisfying and packed with protein. Whether you're winding down after a rigorous workout or seeking a guilt-free indulgence, this mousse will surely hit the spot.

Recipe 71: Sandwich With Peanut Butter and Banana

SERVINGS: 2

PREPPING TIME: 10 MINUTES

COOK TIME: 5 MINUTES

DIFFICULTY: EASY

Indulge in the delectable fusion of peanut butter and banana with this high-protein Instant Pot dessert sandwich. Combining the rich creaminess of peanut butter with the natural sweetness of bananas, it's a delightful treat that's both nutritious and quick to prepare.

Ingredients:

- ✓ 4 slices of whole-grain bread
- ✓ 4 tablespoons of creamy peanut butter
- ✓ 2 ripe bananas, sliced
- ✓ 1 tablespoon of honey (optional)
- ✓ 1/2 teaspoon of cinnamon (optional)

Step-by-Step Preparation:

1. Spread peanut butter evenly on one side of each slice of bread.
2. Arrange banana slices on two of the peanut butter-covered slices.
3. If desired, drizzle with honey and sprinkle with cinnamon.
4. Top with the remaining bread slices, peanut butter side down.
5. Place the sandwiches in the Instant Pot and select the "Steam" function. Cook for 5 minutes.
6. Carefully remove, let cool for a minute, and serve.

Nutritional Facts: (Per serving)

- ❖ Calories: 390
- ❖ Protein: 15g
- ❖ Carbohydrates: 55g
- ❖ Fat: 16g
- ❖ Fiber: 8g
- ❖ Sugar: 21g

This Sandwich With Peanut Butter and Banana is more than just a dessert; it's a protein-packed treat that delivers taste and nutrition. Perfect for those midday hunger pangs or post-workout cravings, this Instant Pot delicacy will have you looking forward to dessert time like never before. Enjoy!

Recipe 72: Sponge Roll With a Protein Souffle

SERVINGS: 4

PREPPING TIME: 20 MINUTES

COOK TIME: 30 MINUTES

DIFFICULTY: MEDIUM

Dive into the delightful fusion of a soft sponge roll filled with a rich protein soufflé. This dessert promises a burst of sweetness and a good dose of protein. Perfect for those who want to satiate sweet tooth while keeping protein intake high. Best of all, it's made effortlessly in an Instant Pot!

Ingredients:

- ✓ 4 large eggs, separated
- ✓ 1/2 cup almond flour
- ✓ 1/4 cup vanilla protein powder
- ✓ 1/4 cup granulated sugar
- ✓ 1 tsp vanilla extract
- ✓ 1/2 tsp cream of tartar
- ✓ Pinch of salt
- ✓ 1/4 cup unsweetened cocoa powder (for the sponge roll)

Step-by-Step Preparation:

1. In a bowl, whip egg whites with cream of tartar until stiff peaks form.
2. Mix egg yolks, sugar, and vanilla extract in another bowl until creamy.
3. Slowly fold almond flour, protein powder, and cocoa into the yolk mixture.
4. Gently fold in the whipped egg whites.
5. Pour batter into a greased Instant Pot-safe dish.
6. Cook on high pressure for 30 minutes. Once done, let it release naturally.
7. Roll the sponge while warm and let it cool.
8. Fill with protein soufflé and roll again. Slice and serve.

Nutritional Facts: (Per serving)

- ❖ Calories: 220 kcal
- ❖ Protein: 14g
- ❖ Carbohydrates: 18g
- ❖ Sugars: 12g
- ❖ Fat: 9g
- ❖ Cholesterol: 185mg

This Sponge Roll with Protein Soufflé is a game-changer for health-conscious dessert enthusiasts. With the power of an Instant Pot, creating this sophisticated dessert is a breeze. Indulge in its airy, light texture while benefiting from a high protein boost. Ideal for post-workout treats or simply when you crave something sweet and nutritious!

Conclusion

Diving into the world of culinary delights, mainly when it centers on a healthy, high-protein diet, can be rewarding and delicious. "High Protein Instant Pot Recipes With Original Photos for Every Dish" isn't just a book; it's a journey. I carefully curated every dish to ensure you never have to sacrifice taste for nutrition.

Beyond just recipes, the visual allure of original photos accompanying each dish inspires both seasoned chefs and novice cooks. Imagine the joy of replicating the very essence of what you see, understanding that every bite contributes to a healthier you. How often do we stumble upon a recipe book that provides us with step-by-step cooking guides and tells a vivid story through its photos? My selection speaks to the soul of every food lover, emphasizing that high-protein meals can be sumptuous and easy to prepare.

Your Instant Pot is more than a kitchen gadget; it's a tool to transform raw ingredients into delightful culinary masterpieces. Each recipe in this collection showcases the versatility of the Instant Pot, making the art of cooking faster and more efficient. You will be armed with a diverse array of meals, from hearty breakfasts to savory dinners, ensuring that every dining experience is unforgettable. My dedication to fostering a fit lifestyle shines through; every recipe is carefully designed to fuel your body without compromising flavor.

So, as you flip back through the pages, remember the power in your hands. You've embarked on a journey to elevate your culinary prowess while embracing a healthy lifestyle. Whether you've been using an Instant Pot for years or just unpacked it from the box, these recipes are tailored for everyone. Begin today, savor every bite, and let each dish be a testament to a healthier, tastier future. Happy cooking!

Printed in Great Britain
by Amazon

42753286R00086